sautéing
new healthy kitchen

RECIPES
Dana Jacobi

GENERAL EDITOR
Chuck Williams

PHOTOGRAPHY
Dan Goldberg

Bonnier
Books

contents

Introduction

8 Eating the rainbow

10 The new healthy kitchen

12 Fruits & vegetables

13 Grains & legumes

14 All about sautéing

16 Creating the healthy meal

18 Purple & blue

23 Purple asparagus with orange
vinaigrette

Purple carrots glazed with red wine

24 Salmon with wild blueberry
& rhubarb sauce

27 Stir-fried pork with black plums

Duck with purple cabbage,
blackberries & port

30 Sichuan beef with aubergine

33 Wild rice with purple pepper
& pecans

Pan-fried blue potatoes with sage

34 Blackberry crêpes

Pomegranate-glazed figs

36 Green

41 Stir-fried chicken with broccoli
& mushrooms

Dry-fried long beans

42 Chicken breasts stuffed with goat's
cheese & rocket

45 Stir-fried calamari & pea shoots

Chicken breasts with tomatillo sauce

48 Fettuccine with fava beans, artichokes
& asparagus

Lemon sole with peas

51 Okra with yellow plum tomatoes

Swiss chard with lemon & anchovy

52 Green figs with almond custard

54 White & tan

59 White asparagus mimosa with
browned butter

Potato galettes with smoked salmon

60 Sicilian prawns with cauliflower & almonds

Potatoes with chorizo & parsley

63 Turkey fricassee with kohlrabi, pears
& mushrooms

Pork chops smothered in onions & apples

66 Mu shu pork

69 Turnips with peas & mushrooms

Chicken with caramelised shallots & wine

70 White nectarines with tawny port

Bananas with cinnamon-chocolate drizzle

Reference

126 Nutrients at work

130 Nutritional values

134 Glossary

139 Bibliography

140 Index

144 Acknowledgements

72 Yellow & orange

77 Spanish tortilla with golden potatoes

78 Prawns with papaya & coconut

Apricot-stuffed chicken breasts

81 Chicken with yellow peppers & passion fruit

Stuffed squash blossoms

84 Swede & golden beetroot with pomegranate seeds

Indian-spiced squash with cashews

87 Ham & sweet potato hash

Butternut squash & pears with rosemary

88 Winter peach shortcake

90 Red

95 Warm tomato & olive bruschetta

Red wine spaghetti with red pepper & onion

96 Sautéed trout with red grape sauce

99 Duck with blood orange sauce

Turkey tenderloin with cranberry compote

102 Rib steak with red wine pan sauce & bronze onions

Sautéed radicchio with pancetta

105 Pork tenderloin with sour cherry sauce

Red-hot hash browns

106 Strawberries in red wine

Toasted pound cake with cherries

108 Brown

113 Ginger couscous with dried fruit

Tamarind shrimp with peanuts

114 Turkey with red mole

117 Cashew chicken stir-fry

120 Mango chicken with toasted quinoa

Kasha with walnuts & pasta

123 Black bean & white corn salad

Lentils with shallots & serrano ham

124 Maple panna cotta with candied walnuts

About this book

This volume of the New Healthy Kitchen was created to teach you how sautéing can be a simple and appealing way to prepare nutrient-rich fruits, vegetables, legumes and grains as well as lean meats, poultry and seafood.

We are fortunate to live in a world where the food we eat has become a choice we can look forward to every day. For some, this means selecting fresh ingredients of all types and incorporating them into well-balanced meals. But it's all too easy to rely on highly processed convenience foods instead. With just a bit of knowledge and know-how, it's easy to choose and prepare healthy options that will increase your energy level and help you to live better.

The recipes in *Sautéing* are organised in a new way: by the colour of the key vegetables or fruits used in the dish. This approach highlights the different nutritional benefits that each colour group contributes to your overall health. If you consume at least one vegetable or fruit from each colour group daily, you can feel confident you are getting the number of servings required for optimum health. Whole grains and legumes have a chapter of their own and, like fresh produce, form the foundation of a wholesome diet.

The New Healthy Kitchen series will help you prepare a wide range of fresh fruits, vegetables and whole grains using a variety of healthy techniques, helping you to bring colour and creativity to every meal you make.

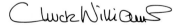

Eating the rainbow

Purple and blue fruits and vegetables contain fibre, vitamins and phytochemicals that promote heart health; help memory function; lower the risk of some cancers; promote urinary tract health; and boost immunity

Green fruits and vegetables contain fibre, vitamins and phytochemicals that lower the risk of breast, prostate, lung and other cancers; promote eye health; help build strong bones and teeth; and boost immunity

White and tan fruits and vegetables contain fibre, vitamins and phytochemicals that promote heart health; help maintain healthful cholesterol levels; lower the risk of breast, lung, and other cancers; and slow cholesterol absorption

Red fruits and vegetables contain fibre, vitamins and phytochemicals that promote heart health; help memory function; lower the risk of certain cancers; promote urinary tract health; and boost immunity

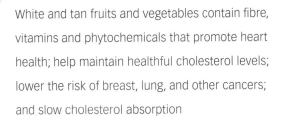

Yellow and orange fruits and vegetables contain fibre, vitamins and phytochemicals that promote heart health; promote eye health; lower the risk of some cancers; and boost immunity

Brown whole grains, legumes, seeds and nuts include fibre, vitamins and phytonutrients that lower blood cholesterol levels and reduce the risk of colon and other cancers, diabetes, heart disease and stroke

Adapted from educational materials of the Produce for Better Health Foundation

The new healthy kitchen

The basic philosophy of the New Healthy Kitchen series is that fresh ingredients, prepared without a lot of fuss, make the most wholesome and enjoyable meals. *Sautéing,* one of three volumes in the series that focuses on a healthy cooking technique, explores one of the easiest and best ways to cook an amazing variety of foods, from vegetables and fruits to grains and legumes.

Healthy food is good food prepared simply to bring out its appealing flavours and presented beautifully to delight the senses. The keys to creating a wholesome meal are to choose the best vegetables and fruits and then to prepare them with an eye to preserving their inherent colours and textures and their valuable nutrients. The recipes in this cookbook promise to bring freshness, colour and variety to your table.

The modern diet is remarkably restricted in the kind of plant foods people eat. With an abundance of all types of food within our reach, we tend to overindulge in concentrated sources of energy, especially animal fats. We also gravitate toward carbohydrates, which are excellent sources of quick energy. But our most common forms of carbohydrates, such as refined flours, are stripped of the vital nutrients found in whole grains. If you can correct such tendencies by making the consumption of fresh produce and whole grains the first priority of your daily diet, you will find that a healthier balance of other foods will follow quite naturally.

Eating fresh plant foods is the ideal way to supply our bodies with the fibre and many of the vitamins and minerals we need for maximum health. Although a multivitamin

or fibre supplement can help fill in the gaps if your diet is lacking, these are not the ideal forms in which to give your body what it needs. Your body can make better use of these compounds when it extracts them in their natural state from different foods. Eating a variety of plant foods is the best way of getting what you need, in a form in which your body is designed to get it.

Some of the benefits of eating fruits and vegetables come from the vitamins, minerals and fibre they contain, but others come from a newly discovered class of nutrients called phytonutrients or phytochemicals. These plant compounds work in a number of ways to protect our bodies and fight disease and in many cases, they are the elements in fruits and

vegetables that give them their distinctive colours and flavours. So the dazzling hues of vegetables and fruits, from red tomatoes to green spinach to purple aubergine, give clues to the particular phytonutrients each contains. Eating a rainbow of produce will give you the broadest array of health benefits from all these various nutrients.

But these fruits and vegetables are not all to consider. Your daily diet must also include members of another group of plant foods: grains and legumes, which are rich in fibre, protein, complex carbohydrates, minerals and phytochemicals. For the most nutritional benefit, use whole grains.

To guide your meal planning, the chapters in this cookbook are organised by the five prominent colour groups of vegetables and

fruits: purple and blue, green, white and tan, yellow and orange and red. A sixth chapter of "brown" foods highlights whole grains, legumes, nuts and seeds. Focusing on the colours of foods when you prepare meals will put a wealth of ingredients, some of them new or overlooked, onto your daily menu. Each colourful chapter begins with a chart showing which fruits and vegetables are at their peak of ripeness each season, helping you vary your diet throughout the year.

The recipes feature a wide range of ingredients and flavours, but are linked by a single cooking technique, sautéing. Simple and quick, these are dishes for busy real-life cooks who want to bring fresh flavours and good health to the dinner table.

Fruits & vegetables

Fruits and vegetables are a cornerstone of a healthy diet. They are also some of the most beautiful and delicious foods on the planet—a gift to both the eye and the palate, with tastes and textures that range from bitter greens to sweet cherries. The recipes in *Sautéing* will inspire you to add new fruits and vegetables to your meals and reap the benefits of their vitamins, minerals and phytochemicals.

In the early years of the twentieth century, scientists discovered the various vitamins and minerals we now know are essential to maintaining good health and fighting disease. Today, we are entering another exciting era of discovery as we learn about the roles that phytochemicals play in the body.

These protective compounds, which are believed to number in the thousands, operate alone and in combination with one another and with nutrients. They work in different ways. For example, some phytochemicals act as antioxidants, protecting the body by neutralising unstable oxygen molecules (known as free radicals) that damage cells and promote disease. Regularly eating plant foods rich in antioxidants is believed to reduce the incidence of various cancers, heart disease, impaired vision and other health problems.

Fruits and vegetables from each of the colour groups provide us with unique combinations of phytonutrients, with each combination playing a unique role in fighting disease and promoting health and well-being. By eating fruits and vegetables at their peak of ripeness and height of nutritional value, you will both please your palate and give your body the benefit of all the healthy nutrients that these flavourful foods contain.

Grains & legumes

Grains and legumes, which are the seeds of plants, contain a wealth of nutrients. They are rich in vitamins and minerals, fibre, protein and phytochemicals, all of which are critical to a healthy, balanced diet. Whole-wheat (wholemeal) bread, grain porridges and stews of peas, beans and lentils have sustained people around the globe since ancient times, proof of the importance of these foods.

But in our modern diet, these nutritional powerhouses too often take a backseat. Our grains are usually refined, in the form of white wheat flour and white rice, with the fibre-rich hull and the nutrient-rich germ milled away. The quantity of whole grains and legumes we consume overall has dropped sharply over the past several decades. Even wholesome carbohydrates—the complex kind—have come under attack by the recent diet fads that demonise all carbohydrates, refined and unrefined.

In the New Healthy Kitchen, recipes emphasising grains, legumes, nuts and seeds are grouped in the Brown chapter. These foods come in a variety of colours,

but you should think of them as brown to remind yourself that they should be as close to their natural state as possible. The superior flavour of whole grains, combined with high nutritional value, makes them equal companions to meats and vegetables.

The sautéed recipes in this book encourage you to try a range of grains, such as amaranth, quinoa and buckwheat, in their whole forms. Fluffy quinoa shines in a role usually played by rice when topped with a tropical blend of mango, chicken, yoghurt and ginger (page 120), while amaranth can be popped like corn for a novel movie-watching snack (page 118). Kasha, or buckwheat groats, mixed with sautéed

onions, pasta and walnuts (page 120), makes a hearty accompaniment to roasted poultry.

Legumes, the seeds of plants with pods that split open when dried, include peas, beans, lentils and peanuts. They contain fibre, complex carbohydrates and some iron, plus enough protein that they can substitute for meat, fish or poultry, allowing you to enjoy the occasional meatless meal.

Other seeds, such as flaxseeds, sesame seeds and nuts, can add flavour, texture, colour and excellent nutrition to recipes. Cashews, for instance, hold their own in a stir-fry with chicken (page 117) and a medley of seeds makes a delicious garnish for breakfast yoghurt or cereal (page 119).

All about sautéing

Sautéing is an ideal technique for the New Healthy Kitchen because it cooks food quickly, preserving its flavours, and by not diluting them in liquid, preserving its nutrients. By intensifying the flavours in foods, sautéing increases the pleasure of eating healthy vegetables, fruits and even grains. Although generally used for main dishes, this cooking method is also good for making starters, sides and desserts.

Sautéing calls for cooking food rapidly over high heat in a small amount of fat. The technique—the name of which derives from the French word for "jump"—has been traditionally described as tossing and stirring small pieces of food in a hot pan. The definition has expanded to include larger pieces of fish, poultry and meat, which are sometimes cut or pounded thin to keep the cooking time short. These larger pieces don't need to be kept moving constantly, though are sometimes turned several times.

Since there is no water involved, sautéing is known as a dry-heat cooking method, like grilling and roasting. The dry heat and fat create appealing and delicious browning.

As food browns, its juices concentrate and caramelise. Adding liquid to the pan at the end of sautéing dissolves these juices and produces a delicious sauce in minutes. Successful sautéing requires a heavy-bottomed pan that conducts heat evenly. Enamelled steel, lined copper, high-quality non-stick, and cast iron are all good choices for materials. You can use either a shallow frying pan with sloping sides or a deeper sauté pan with straight sides, depending on what you are cooking.

It is important to select a pan size that holds the food comfortably. If the pan is too small, the liquid will collect rather than evaporate and the food will steam rather than sear. If the pan is too big, both the food and pan will dry out too quickly and possibly scorch or even burn.

As a rule, start sautéing over medium-high or high heat, to ensure a nice browned surface, and then lower the heat so that the food will cook through without burning.

To lessen the risk of foods sticking to the pan, always heat the pan before you add the fat, and then heat the fat before you add the food. Swirl the pan to coat it evenly with the fat. When sautéing a larger piece of poultry or meat, let it cook undisturbed for a few minutes to brown well on the first side.

There are a few variations on sautéing. Dry sautéing uses no fat and is particularly good for fruits and onions, giving the foods an appealing flavour and colour by searing the surface but not cooking them through. Wet sautéing in a bit of broth is another way of concentrating flavours without using fat. Shallow frying uses more fat than typical sautéing but far less than deep-frying. It makes foods like potatoes golden and crisp.

Stir-frying, a form of sautéing that originated in Asia, calls for cooking small pieces of food in a little oil over the highest possible heat. A flat-bottomed wok works best on conventional stoves because it conducts heat well and evenly. A large, deep, heavy frying pan can also be used. All of your ingredients must be chopped and your sauce ingredients combined before you start to cook because the cooking goes quite quickly. To test the oil, flick a drop of water into the pan; it should sizzle. As you cook, keep the food moving constantly.

The best fats for sautéing are healthy ones which won't burn easily. Rape seed and grape seed oils are rich in mono- and polyunsaturated fats that help lower the level of bad cholesterol and increase the good cholesterol. Olive oil has a lower smoke point but is healthy as well. For stir-fries, beneficial peanut oil heats well and gives a traditional Asian flavor, while sesame oil can be used as a seasoning if not a cooking medium. Butter, used in moderation, adds delicious flavour to sautéed dishes.

Creating the healthy meal

A commitment to eating a healthy diet based on vegetables, fruits, legumes and whole grains may mean making some lifestyle changes. For example, you might need to modify your shopping habits, visiting the market once a week or more often for seasonal fresh produce, or to reduce portions of meat if you've grown accustomed to large portions. But the rewards will be evident quickly.

To find the best fresh produce, seek out just-harvested, locally grown vegetables and fruits in season at a good produce market or a natural-foods store. Or better yet, make a visit to a farmers' market one of your weekend outings. Although organic produce costs more, pesticide-free fruits and vegetables picked at the peak of ripeness at local farms also taste better and are more densely packed with nutrients.

The colourful eating philosophy of the New Healthy Kitchen emphasises plant foods, but it doesn't exclude a variety of meats and dairy products. These ingredients add flavour, interest, texture and nutrients to a wide selection of healthy dishes.

Meat, dairy and other animal foods appeal to our bodies' craving for nutrient-rich calories, but it is easy to overindulge in these items, especially when you lead a typically sedentary modern life. The secret is to find balance in using and enjoying these ingredients. Animal foods contribute important proteins and vitamins to the diet, so they have a place in the New Healthy Kitchen. But they should play a co-starring role alongside vegetables and grains, rather than dominating the dinner plate. Always keep your servings modest: a reasonable portion of cooked, boneless meat, poultry or seafood is about the size of a deck of playing cards. Remember, too, that certain cuts of meats and many cheeses can act as additional seasoning elements, rather than main events.

While excessive fat adds unnecessary calories to the diet, a certain amount of fat is essential for the body to function properly. Fat also gives us the sensation of being satiated, which helps us to avoid overeating. Most of the recipes in this book use olive, rape and grape seed oils as the primary fats for sautéing. These oils have been proven beneficial, thanks to their mono-unsaturated fat content, which raises the level of good cholesterol and lowers the bad.

Herbs and spices are absolutely essential as flavour boosters in healthy dishes. A simple scattering of chopped fresh parsley or citrus zest adds both colour and an intense flavour note to many different foods and anti-oxidants as well. Vinegar and citrus juice are other important flavourings in the New Healthy Kitchen. These ingredients contribute an acidic note to a dish, which boosts other flavours without adding fat and making a dish heavy.

The simple act of cooking meals at home for ourselves and our loved ones instead of loading up on take-away and restaurant food is a great step toward healthy eating. The recipes in the New Healthy Kitchen are deliberately easy and streamlined. Preparation and cooking times are listed at the beginning of the recipe to help you fit it into your daily routine. Many main dishes can be prepared in half an hour or a little more, making them perfect for a midweek family supper. The more frequently you shop and cook, the more of a habit it becomes, even in the midst of a busy day-to-day life. And the rewards are great. Eating meals at home is often the highlight of the day. It bonds couples and families together and makes us appreciate all the wonderful foods nature has provided for us.

purple kale prunes blueberries

PURPLE AND BLUE FRUITS AND VEGETABLES PROMOTE

blackcurrants purple carrots

MEMORY FUNCTION • HELP PROMOTE URINARY TRACT

lavender blackberries purple

HEALTH • BOOST THE IMMUNE SYSTEM • HELP PROMOTE

cabbage raisins black grapes

HEALTHY AGEING • OFFER ANTIOXIDANTS FOR HEALING

purple figs blue plums purple

AND PROTECTION • HELP REDUCE THE RISK OF SOME

peppers purple radishes

CANCERS • PURPLE AND BLUE FRUITS AND VEGETABLES

Purple & blue

Deep-coloured blueberries, aubergines, purple cabbages, black plums—the well-known purple and blue fruits and vegetables of the produce world are stunning on almost any plate. But you'll discover quickly that some family members that are better known in other shades, such as purple asparagus, carrots and potatoes and dusky sweet peppers, are equally appealing.

All the purple and blue vegetables and fruits are gems because they are both alluring to the senses and packed with potent health benefits. Their intense and unusual colour—a sure sign of abundant antioxidants that protect the heart and memory—can add vivid hues to sautés and stir-fries all year round.

In spring, purple asparagus and sautéed shallots are served in a warm citrus dressing (page 23), while on a balmy summer night, the sweet-tart flavours of wild blueberries and rhubarb are the perfect foil for salmon fillet quickly seared in a hot pan, the fish delivering both beneficial omega-3 fatty acids and delicious flavour (page 24). When the weather cools, a lean duck breast, served over sautéed purple cabbage seasoned with the warm flavours of rosemary and ginger, goes well with a robust red wine (page 27), or panfried blue potatoes topped with crisp sage leaves prove themselves to be the perfect partner for a thick veal chop or a tender rib-eye steak (page 33).

SPRING	SUMMER	AUTUMN	WINTER
purple asparagus	purple peppers	purple-tipped Belgian endive	purple-tipped Belgian endive
purple-tipped Belgian endive	blackberries	purple peppers	purple cabbage
blueberries	blueberries	blueberries	purple carrots
purple cabbage	fresh blackcurrants	purple cabbage	currants
purple carrots	aubergines	purple carrots	blue, purple & black grapes
currants	purple figs	currants	black olives
blue, purple & black grapes	lavender	aubergines	blue potatoes
prunes	blue, purple & black plums	purple figs	prunes
raisins	purple and black tomatoes	blue, purple & black grapes	raisins
purple radishes		blue, purple & black plums	
		blue potatoes	
		prunes	
		raisins	

purple asparagus with orange vinaigrette

14 spears fat purple or green asparagus (about 500 g/1 lb), tough ends trimmed

½ tsp olive oil

2 tsp finely chopped shallot

Juice of 1 navel orange

1 Tbsp lime juice

1 tsp lavender honey

2 Tbsp fresh chervil leaves for garnish (optional)

Cut asparagus tips on the diagonal and set aside. Cut 10 stalks on the diagonal into slices 6 mm (¼ in) thick. Using a vegetable peeler, remove the coloured outside of the remaining 4 stalks in long strips. Discard interior of the spears or reserve for another use.

Blanch asparagus tips and strips in boiling water for 30 seconds. Remove with a slotted spoon and cool in ice water. Spin in a salad spinner or pat dry with paper towels.

Heat oil in a non-stick frying pan over medium-high heat. Add shallot and sauté until starting to soften, about 30 seconds. Add citrus juices, then stir in honey until it dissolves. Remove pan from heat.

To serve, arrange asparagus slices and shaved strips on 4 salad plates. Spoon on warm dressing and garnish with chervil, if using.

To prepare: 10 minutes

To cook: 3 minutes

4 starter or side-dish servings

purple carrots glazed with red wine

2 tsp butter or rape seed oil

24 young, slender purple or orange carrots

125 ml (4 fl oz) fruity red wine such as Beaujolais

80 ml (3 fl oz) low-salt chicken stock

1 tsp peppercorns, coarsely cracked

Melt butter or heat oil in a non-stick frying pan over medium-high heat. Add carrots, stir to coat, and cook for 2 minutes. Add wine, stock and peppercorns. Reduce heat to medium and cook until most of the liquid has evaporated and carrots are fork-tender, about 10 minutes. Serve carrots hot or warm.

Note: Since their purple colour and many of their nutrients are in the skin, do not peel carrots. If only large carrots are available, cut them on the diagonal into slices 12 mm (½ in) thick.

To prepare: 5 minutes

To cook: 12 minutes

4 side-dish servings

salmon with wild blueberry & rhubarb sauce

Blueberry & Rhubarb Sauce

1 Tbsp rape seed oil

1 small onion, cut in half, halves cut into slices

2–3 thin stalks rhubarb, about 180 g (6 oz), cut into slices 12 mm (½ in) thick

185 g (6 oz) fresh or frozen wild or cultivated blueberries

2 Tbsp blueberry or wildflower honey

125 ml (4 fl oz) unsweetened blueberry juice (optional; see Note)

¼ tsp wasabi powder or paste

500 g (1 lb) salmon fillet, cut crossways into 4 equal pieces

For Sauce: Heat oil in a sauté pan over medium-high heat. Add onion and sauté until lightly browned, 4–5 minutes. Add rhubarb and cook, stirring, until bottom of pan looks syrupy, 3–4 minutes. Add blueberries and honey. Add blueberry juice if using frozen berries. When berries start to soften, after about 1 minute, lower heat to medium. Simmer until rhubarb is tender and collapsing, about 5 minutes. Remove from heat and stir in wasabi. Transfer to a bowl and cover to keep warm.

Heat a dry non-stick frying pan over medium heat until hot. Sprinkle fish with ½ tsp salt and ⅛ tsp pepper. Arrange salmon in pan and cook until browned and crisp on bottom, about 4 minutes. Using a wide spatula, turn salmon and brown on second side, about 3 minutes, lowering heat if necessary to prevent burning. Fish should flake easily with a fork and still be translucent in the centre only.

To serve, divide fish among warmed plates, spoon sauce in the centre of each plate and place fish on top of the sauce.

Note: If using fresh wild berries, include the blueberry juice. Fresh wild blueberries contain less moisture than cultivated ones or frozen ones.

To prepare: 10 minutes

To cook: 20 minutes

4 servings

stir-fried pork with black plums

1 tsp hoisin sauce

1 Tbsp lime juice

2 tsp cornflour

2 tsp rape seed oil

375 g (12 oz) pork tenderloin, sliced on diagonal 12 mm (½ in) thick

125 ml (4 fl oz) apple juice

¼ tsp grated fresh ginger

1 small jalapeño chilli, seeded and cut lengthways into thin strips

2 large black plums, halved, stoned, and cut into 12-mm (½-in) wedges

In a small bowl, mix together hoisin sauce, lime juice and cornflour. Set hoisin mixture aside.

Heat oil in a large frying pan over medium-high heat. Brown pork slices, turning once, 6–8 minutes total. Transfer meat to a plate. Add apple juice, ginger and chilli to pan and stir to scrape up browned bits. Boil until liquid is reduced by one-third, about 3 minutes. Add plums and hoisin mixture and return pork to pan. Stir until sauce thickens, coating meat, about 3 minutes. Arrange pork on a warmed serving platter, spoon sauce over and serve at once.

Note: Serve with sautéed or steamed spinach.

To prepare: 15 minutes

To cook: 12 minutes

4 servings

duck with purple cabbage, blackberries & port

2 Tbsp plus 1 tsp rape seed oil

1 head (about 875 g/1¾ lb) purple cabbage, shredded

160 ml (5 fl oz) unsweetened black cherry juice

80 ml (3 fl oz) ruby port

1 Tbsp ginger marmalade or orange marmalade

1 tsp chopped fresh rosemary

125 g (4 oz) fresh or frozen blackberries

1 whole boneless duck breast, about 625 g (1¼ lb)

Preheat oven to 230°C (450°F). Heat 2 Tbsp oil in a medium sauté pan over medium-high heat. Add cabbage and sauté until wilted, about 5 minutes. Stir in cherry juice, port, marmalade and rosemary and cook until cabbage is soft and most of liquid has evaporated, about 15 minutes. Add berries and cook until heated through, about 2 minutes more. (This can be done 1 day ahead; reheat cabbage, covered, in a preheated 180°C/350°F oven.)

Heat remaining 1 tsp oil in an ovenproof frying pan over medium heat. Add duck, skin side down and sauté until skin is browned and the fat is rendered, about 12 minutes. Discard fat and turn duck. Place pan in oven and cook until a meat thermometer inserted into thickest part of duck registers 65°C (150°F), about 12 minutes. (It must be served rare, or it will be tough.) Remove to a board and rest for 10 minutes.

Arrange cabbage on a warmed serving platter. Remove and discard duck skin. Cut breast crossways into slices 6 mm (¼ in) thick and arrange over cabbage. Serve at once.

To prepare: 15 minutes

To cook: 60 minutes

6 servings

savoury & spicy blackberry sauce

After sautéing pork or turkey, add 125 ml (4 fl oz) blackcurrant juice and a finely chopped shallot to pan over medium heat and deglaze. Add blackberries and a pinch of chipotle chilli powder. Cook for 1 minute, and serve over meat.

aubergine caponata

Sauté diced red onion and aubergine in olive oil until softened. Add chopped tomato, raisins, capers, a dash of vinegar and a smear of tomato paste. When aubergine is tender, season with salt and pepper. Serve at room temperature.

purple cabbage with raisins

Sauté shredded purple cabbage in melted butter until limp. Add a handful of raisins, 1 or 2 cinnamon sticks, honey, a splash of balsamic vinegar, apple cider as needed to moisten and salt and pepper. Cook until tender-crisp, then serve warm.

blueberries with lemon

Warm 125 g (4 oz) fresh or frozen berries in butter. Add plenty of wild blueberry juice, a splash of lemon liqueur and 1 tsp cornflour. Boil, stirring, until sauce is clear. Serve lukewarm over sliced madeira cake.

sichuan beef
with aubergine

375 g (12 oz) skirt steak

375 g (12 oz) slender aubergines

2 tsp sugar

60 ml (2 fl oz) low-salt
chicken stock

2 Tbsp low-sodium soy sauce

2 Tbsp sherry

2 tsp rice wine vinegar

4 Tbsp peanut oil

3 Tbsp chopped garlic

45 g (1½ oz) chopped spring
onions, including white and
tender green parts

Steamed brown rice for serving

2 Tbsp chopped fresh
coriander for garnish

Freeze meat for up to 1 hour to make it easier to slice. Thinly slice with the grain, then cut slices into pieces 5 cm (2 ins) long. Set aside.

Trim aubergines and cut on the diagonal into slices 12 mm (½ in) thick. Stack and cut slices lengthways into thirds. Set aside.

In a small bowl, mix together sugar, stock, soy sauce, sherry, vinegar and ¼ tsp pepper. Set aside.

Heat oil in a wok over medium-high heat until almost smoking. Using a slotted spoon, transfer beef to hot oil. Stir-fry until colour changes, about 1½ minutes. Remove to a plate using a slotted spoon. Add garlic and spring onions to wok and stir-fry until fragrant, about 30 seconds. Remove to plate with beef. Pour off all but 2 Tbsp oil and add aubergine. Stir-fry until it starts to soften, about 2 minutes. Add soy sauce mixture and cook until aubergine is tender, about 2 minutes more.

Return beef, garlic and spring onions to wok. When beef is cooked through, about 2 minutes, spoon hot stir-fry hot over rice and garnish with coriander. Serve at once.

*To prepare: 35 minutes,
plus 1 hour to freeze meat*

To cook: 8 minutes

*4 main-course servings,
6 with other dishes*

wild rice with purple pepper & pecans

2 Tbsp peanut oil

1 medium purple or green pepper, seeded and diced

1 small red onion, chopped

250g (8oz) cooked wild rice, frozen and thawed (see Note)

½ tsp grated orange zest

30 g (1 oz) coarsely chopped pecans

Heat oil in a wok over medium-high heat until almost smoking. Add pepper and onion and stir-fry until onion is translucent, about 2 minutes. Add rice and orange zest and stir-fry until rice is heated through, about 1½ minutes. Stir in pecans. Serve hot or warm.

Note: Freezing rice reduces sticking when it is stir-fried.

To prepare: 10 minutes

To cook: 4 minutes

4 side-dish servings

pan-fried blue potatoes with sage

375 g (12 oz) small blue or red new potatoes

4 Tbsp olive oil

10 medium fresh sage leaves

In a saucepan, cover potatoes with 5 cm (2 ins) cold water. Bring to the boil over high heat and cook until a thin knife inserted into potatoes meets only slight resistance, about 20 minutes. Drain potatoes and pat dry. Slice potatoes 1 cm (⅜ in) thick, discarding any loose skin.

Heat oil in a medium sauté pan over medium-high heat. Arrange potatoes in a single layer, leaving 6 mm (¼ in) between slices (you may need to cook them in 2 batches). Cook potatoes, turning once, until golden and crusty on both sides, 8–9 minutes total. Remove potatoes with slotted spoon and drain on paper towels, blotting dry.

Add sage leaves to pan; they will sizzle and curl slightly. In 10 seconds, turn leaves with tongs and fry for 5 seconds more. Drain sage on fresh paper towels.

Arrange potatoes on a warmed platter, sprinkle with 1 tsp salt, and top with sage leaves. Serve at once.

To prepare: 5 minutes

To cook: 30 minutes

6 starter servings or 4 side-dish servings

blackberry crêpes

Buckwheat Crêpes

60 g (2 oz) buckwheat flour

60 g (2 oz) plain flour

125 g (4 oz) plus 2 tsp sugar

250 ml (8 fl oz) whole or reduced-fat milk

1 large egg plus 1 large egg white

¼ tsp salt

2 Tbsp clarified butter (see Note, page 96)

60 g (2 oz) Neufchâtel or low-fat cream cheese

60 ml (2 fl oz) low-fat or whole plain yoghurt

1 Tbsp limoncello or other lemon liqueur

185 g (6 oz) fresh or unthawed frozen blackberries

125 g (4 oz) sugar

For Crêpes: Whisk together flours, sugar, milk, whole egg, egg white and salt in a bowl until smooth. Leave batter to stand for at least 30 minutes, or cover and refrigerate for up to 24 hours. Heat 2 tsp butter in a medium crêpe pan or medium frying pan over medium-high heat. When very hot, pour in a scant 80 ml (3 fl oz) batter and quickly tilt pan to cover bottom evenly. Cook until crêpe is dark brown on bottom, about 3 minutes. Flip and cook on second side for 1 minute. Repeat to make 8 crêpes in all, brushing pan with more butter as needed. Stack cooked, cooled crêpes on a plate. If not using at once, cover with foil and leave to stand for up to 2 hours or refrigerate for up to 24 hours.

Combine cheese, yoghurt, and liqueur in mini-food processor or blender and process to make a filling. If not using at once, cover and refrigerate (for up to 2 days).

To serve, wrap crêpes in foil and reheat in a 95°C (200°F) oven for 10 minutes. (If crêpes have been refrigerated, reheat for 15 minutes in a 180°C/ 350°F oven.) Fold each crêpe in half, spread with filling and fold into quarters. Place 2 crêpes on each of 4 dessert plates. Combine blackberries and sugar in a medium non-stick frying pan over medium heat and sauté until berries are slightly soft and surrounded by syrup, about 3 minutes. Spoon hot berries and syrup over crêpes and serve.

To prepare: 20 minutes, plus 30 minutes to stand

To cook: 25–30 minutes

4 dessert servings

pomegranate-glazed figs

2 tsp butter

8 fresh purple figs stemmed and halved lengthways

125 ml (4 fl oz) pomegranate juice

3 whole cloves

2 Tbsp mascarpone cheese

Unsweetened cocoa powder to decorate (see Note)

Melt butter in a medium frying pan over medium-high heat. Add figs, cut side down and sauté until golden, about 4 minutes. Using tongs, turn figs and cook for 1 minute more. Arrange 4 fig halves on each of 4 dessert plates, with bottoms toward the centre to make a star.

Add pomegranate juice and cloves to pan and boil until liquid is syrupy, about 5 minutes. Discard cloves and spoon warm syrup over figs. Place 1½ tsp cheese in centre of each plate and sprinkle with cocoa powder. Serve figs warm.

Note: Sprinkle cocoa powder using an icing sugar shaker or by putting it in a sieve and gently tapping it.

To prepare: 5 minutes

To cook: 10 minutes

4 dessert servings

avocados pea shoots spinach

GREEN FRUITS AND VEGETABLES BOOST THE IMMUNE

watercress rocket asparagus

SYSTEM • PROMOTE EYE HEALTH • HELP BUILD STRONG

kale broccoli snow peas leeks

BONES • BUILD STRONG TEETH • OFFER ANTIOXIDANTS

lettuce courgettes green beans

FOR HEALING AND PROTECTION • REDUCE THE RISK OF

endive brussels sprouts limes

CERTAIN CANCERS • GREEN FRUITS AND VEGETABLES

green tea kiwifruits artichokes

BOOST THE IMMUNE SYSTEM • PROMOTE EYE HEALTH

Green

It is easy to eat members of this big family: green, nature's most frequent colour, includes a broad variety of vegetables and fruits, all of which supply important health benefits. Enjoy at least one serving from the group at every meal, choosing from leafy dark greens and tender lettuces, green apples and figs, cruciferous broccoli and cabbage, creamy avocados and more.

Green vegetables range in flavour from tangy tomatillos, crispy rocket and robust broccoli to delicate pea shoots and sweet sugar snaps—in other words, a taste to complement every meal.

In this chapter, you'll find chicken breasts stuffed with rocket and goat's cheese served with a quick sauté of tomatoes and leeks (page 42), a pleasing pairing of contrasting red and green. You'll also discover an enlightened stir-fry that marries calamari rings with tender green pea shoots and spring onions (page 45).

Classic French cooking is seldom labelled healthy, but green peas and tender lettuce sautéed in a modest amount of butter and then showered with a chiffonade of fresh mint prove that it can be just that (page 47).

For breakfast or dessert, reach for green grapes, kiwifruits and green apples and pears. Or sauté green figs in a tiny nugget of butter and serve them in a shallow pool of almond custard for a dessert that is both delicious and healthy (page 52).

SPRING	SUMMER	AUTUMN	WINTER
artichokes	rocket	green apples	green apples
asparagus	avocados (Hass)	artichokes	avocados (Fuerte)
green peppers	green chillis	bok choy	bok choy
endive	cucumbers	broccoli	broccoli
green beans	green beans	sprouting broccoli	sprouting broccoli
limes	spring onions	Brussels sprouts	Brussels sprouts
lettuce	herbs	green cabbage	green cabbage
green pears	limes	endive	celery
mangetout peas	green-fleshed melons	green grapes	endive
snow peas	okra	kale	kale
pea shoots	sugar snap peas	leeks	leeks
sugar snap peas	spinach	green pears	snow peas
spinach	tomatillos	Swiss chard	spinach
watercress	courgettes	watercress	watercress

stir-fried chicken with broccoli & mushrooms

1 Tbsp fermented black beans

2 Tbsp dry sherry

250 g (8 oz) finely chopped chicken breast

⅛ tsp ground white pepper

1 tsp Asian sesame oil

10 g (⅓ oz) fresh Thai basil leaves

2 Tbsp peanut or rape seed oil

2 Tbsp chopped garlic

1 Tbsp chopped fresh ginger

185 g (6 oz) broccoli florets

60 g (2 oz) chopped shallots

2 Tbsp low-salt chicken stock

1 tin (470 g/15 oz) straw mushrooms, drained

Cooked rice noodles to serve

In a small bowl, soak black beans in sherry for 20 minutes. Drain, reserving sherry. In another bowl, mix chicken with ½ tsp salt, white pepper and sesame oil and cover with cling film. Leave the chicken to stand for 20 minutes.

Stack the basil leaves and roll up lengthways. With a sharp knife, cut crossways into thin strips to make a chiffonade for garnish. Set aside.

Heat peanut oil in a wok over medium-high heat until almost smoking. Add chicken and stir-fry, breaking up meat with a spatula, until colour changes from pink to brown, about 2 minutes. Remove chicken to a plate using a slotted spoon. Add garlic, ginger and black beans and stir-fry until fragrant, about 30 seconds. Add broccoli and shallots and stir-fry for 1 minute. Add stock, reserved sherry and ½ tsp salt and stir to combine. Return chicken to wok, add mushrooms and stir-fry until wok is almost dry, 2–3 minutes.

To serve, spoon noodles into bowls or onto a platter and top with chicken and vegetables. Garnish with basil and serve at once.

To prepare: 10 minutes, plus 20 minutes to soak and marinate

To cook: 6 minutes

4 servings

dry-fried long beans

60 ml (2 fl oz) low-salt chicken stock

1 tsp sugar

125 ml (4 fl oz) rape seed oil

375 g (12 oz) long beans, cut into 10-cm (4-in) lengths

2 Tbsp finely chopped fresh ginger

1 red pepper, seeded and chopped

1 Tbsp balsamic vinegar

1 tsp Asian sesame oil (see Note)

In small bowl, mix together stock, sugar and ½ tsp salt. Set aside.

Heat oil in a wok over medium-high heat until almost smoking. Add beans and cook, alternately stirring them and pressing them against pan, until skin wrinkles and brown spots appear, about 3 minutes. Remove beans to a plate using a slotted spoon. Pour off all but 1 Tbsp oil. Return wok to medium-high heat, add ginger and stir-fry until fragrant, about 30 seconds. Add stock mixture, return beans to wok and cook until wok is almost dry, 3–4 minutes. Stir in pepper, vinegar and sesame oil. Serve warm or at room temperature.

Note: Use the dark brown, aromatic Japanese or Chinese sesame oil made with roasted sesame seeds.

To prepare: 10 minutes

To cook: 8 minutes

4–6 side-dish servings

chicken breasts stuffed with goat's cheese & rocket

250 g (8 oz) coarsely chopped rocket, rinsed and shaken

4 skinless, boneless chicken breasts about 185 g (6 oz) each

90 g (3 oz) creamy fresh goat's cheese

Sauce

2 Tbsp olive oil

60 g (2 oz) chopped leek, white part only

30 g (1 oz) finely chopped red onion

1 clove garlic, finely chopped

470 g (15 oz) seeded and chopped plum (Roma) tomatoes

250 g (8 oz) tinned chopped tomatoes

60 ml (2 fl oz) dry white wine such as Pinot Grigio or Sancerre

Cook damp rocket in a dry, non-stick frying pan over medium-high heat until it wilts and is dark green, about 3 minutes. Remove rocket to a plate and leave to cool.

While rocket cools, pound each breast between 2 sheets of cling film, using a mallet or rolling pin, until 6 mm (¼ in) thick.

Squeeze water from rocket and chop finely. In a bowl, combine chopped rocket with goat's cheese, ½ tsp salt and a few grindings pepper. Place quarter of goat's cheese mixture in centre of each breast, spreading it with your fingers over the breast and leaving a 6 mm (¼ in) border uncovered all around. Starting at a narrow end, roll up each breast like a swiss roll. Set stuffed breasts, seam side down, on a plate and cover with cling film.

For Sauce: Heat oil in a sauté pan over medium-high heat. Add leek and onion and sauté until onion is translucent, about 4 minutes. Add garlic and sauté for 1 minute more. Add plum tomatoes with their liquid and sauté until they start to soften, 3–4 minutes. Add tinned tomatoes, cover and simmer for 5 minutes.

Add stuffed chicken breasts to pan, cover and cook over medium heat until opaque all the way through, 15–20 minutes. With tongs, remove chicken to a warmed serving platter and tent with foil. Add wine to sauce and cook over medium-high heat until it has a chunky, light consistency, about 5 minutes.

Serve chicken rolls, whole or sliced, with sauce spooned alongside.

To prepare: 30 minutes, plus 15 minutes to cool

To cook: 40 minutes

4 servings

stir-fried calamari & pea shoots

500 g (1 lb) green pea shoots

375 g (12 oz) cleaned squid bodies

4 Tbsp peanut or rape seed oil

2 Tbsp finely chopped garlic

1 Tbsp finely chopped fresh ginger

45 g (1½ oz) chopped spring onions, green part only

60 ml (2 fl oz) chicken stock

1 Tbsp low-sodium soy sauce

1 tsp Asian chilli paste

1 tsp sugar

1 tsp Asian sesame oil

Steamed brown rice to serve

Rinse pea shoots, remove and discard tough parts, and dry thoroughly. Set aside. Cut squid into 2-cm (¾-in) rings and set aside.

Heat 2 Tbsp peanut oil in a wok over medium-high heat. Add garlic and ginger and stir-fry until fragrant, about 30 seconds. Add pea shoots and spring onions and stir-fry until volume is reduced by half, 3 minutes. Add stock, ½ tsp salt and ⅛ tsp pepper and cook until shoots are tender-crisp, about 2 minutes. Remove to a plate with a slotted spoon.

Wipe out wok. In a small bowl, mix together soy sauce, chilli paste, sugar and sesame oil. Heat 2 Tbsp peanut oil in wok over medium-high heat. Add squid and stir-fry until opaque, about 2 minutes. Return pea shoots to wok, add soy sauce mixture, and stir-fry, tossing to combine and heat through, about 1 minute. Using a slotted spoon, remove greens and squid to serving platter. Serve hot over brown rice.

To prepare: 15 minutes

To cook: 9 minutes

4 servings

chicken breasts with tomatillo sauce

1 Tbsp rape seed oil

2 shallots, chopped

2 spring onions, white part only, chopped

1 serrano chilli, seeded and finely chopped

3 medium tomatillos, chopped

15 g (½ oz) fresh coriander leaves

1 tsp dried oregano

125 ml (4 fl oz) chicken stock

1 Tbsp lime juice

4 skinless, boneless chicken breasts 125 g (4 oz) each

Heat oil in a medium frying pan over medium-high heat. Sauté shallots until translucent, about 4 minutes. Add spring onions and chilli, cook for 1 minute. Add tomatillos, half the coriander and the oregano and sauté until tomatillos are soft, about 4 minutes. Add chicken stock and continue to cook until most of liquid has evaporated, about 5 minutes. Remove contents of pan to a blender, add lime juice, and process to a pulpy purée, making about 250 ml (8 fl oz) sauce. Set aside.

Pound each breast between 2 sheets of cling film, using a meat pounder, until 6 mm (¼ in) thick. Season with salt and pepper. Heat a heavy non-stick frying pan over medium-high heat. Sear chicken in dry pan until opaque throughout, turning breasts once, 5 minutes total.

To serve, place chicken on warmed dinner plates and spoon sauce over. Garnish with remaining coriander. Pass remaining sauce in a jug.

To prepare: 20 minutes

To cook: 20 minutes

4 servings

chinese broccoli with oyster sauce

Steam Chinese broccoli for 3 minutes. In a wok, stir-fry chopped fresh ginger for 30 seconds. Add broccoli, 1 tsp sugar and 1 Tbsp chicken stock. Stir-fry for 1 minute more. Drizzle with oyster sauce and serve.

french peas & lettuce

Cut a head of butter lettuce into quarters. Sauté in butter with petits pois until lettuce wilts. Add 125 ml (4 fl oz) chicken stock and cook until lettuce is tender. Season with salt and pepper, sprinkle with chopped mint and serve.

brussels sprouts with capers & lemon

Sauté thinly sliced sprouts in oil until bright green. Add a generous splash of chicken stock and continue cooking until sprouts are tender-crisp. Mix in rinsed capers, some lemon zest, a squirt of lemon juice, salt and pepper.

garlic spinach

Purée 2 garlic cloves with 250 ml (8 fl oz) water. Cut Savoy or regular spinach, including tender stems, into wide strips and sauté in olive oil until wilted. Add garlic water. Cook until tender. Season with salt and pepper.

fettuccine with broad beans, artichokes & asparagus

1 lemon

625 g (1¼ lb) baby artichokes

500 g (1 lb) fresh broad beans, shelled

8 spears thin asparagus, tough ends trimmed, spears cut into 5-cm (2-in) pieces

3 Tbsp olive oil

2 cloves garlic, sliced lengthways

375 g (12 oz) dried farro or whole-wheat fettuccine

30 g (1 oz) grated pecorino cheese

Squeeze lemon into large bowl and add squeezed halves and 500 ml (16 fl oz) water. Cut off top of each artichoke, discard outer leaves, trim base and add to lemon water. When all are trimmed, pour 250 ml (8 fl oz) lemon water into steamer pan, put artichokes, broad beans and asparagus on rack, cover, bring to boil, and steam until tender, about 6 minutes. Return vegetables to lemon water to cool, then drain. Halve artichokes lengthways and slip thick skins from the broad beans.

Heat oil in a frying pan over medium-high heat. Add garlic and sauté until golden, about 4 minutes. Remove to a plate with a slotted spoon. Sauté artichokes in garlic oil until warmed through, about 3 minutes. Add favas and asparagus and sauté for 2–3 minutes more.

Meanwhile, cook pasta in salted boiling water until al dente, 12 minutes. Drain pasta and divide among warmed wide, shallow bowls. Spoon vegetables and oil over pasta, top with garlic and cheese and serve.

To prepare: 30 minutes

To cook: 25 minutes

4 servings

lemon sole with peas

125 g (4 oz) sugar snap peas

155 g (5 oz) fresh or frozen baby green peas

4 sole fillets, 185 g (6 oz) each

60 g (2 oz) plain flour

2 Tbsp clarified butter (see Note, page 96)

Juice of 1 lemon

2 Tbsp dry white wine such as Sauvignon Blanc or dry Riesling

Blanch sugar snap peas for 30 seconds in boiling water. Add green peas and cook for 30 seconds more. Drain peas, remove to a warmed serving platter, tent with foil and set aside.

Pat fish dry with paper towels. Season to taste with salt and pepper. Dredge in flour and gently tap and shake off excess. Heat clarified butter in a frying pan just large enough to hold fish. Shaking pan, add fillets, placing the more attractive side down. Continue shaking for 1 minute to prevent sticking. Cook until fish is golden, 1–2 minutes. Using a wide spatula, turn fish and cook, shaking pan or sliding spatula underneath to keep it from sticking, until almost opaque in centre at thickest point, 2–4 minutes. Arrange fish on top of peas.

Add lemon juice and wine to pan and stir to scrape up browned bits. Spoon hot sauce over fish and serve at once.

To prepare: 8 minutes

To cook: 8 minutes

4 servings

okra with yellow plum tomatoes

1 Tbsp olive oil

60 g (2 oz) chopped onion

250 g (8 oz) okra, sliced crossways 12 mm (½ in) thick

3 yellow plum tomatoes, halved lengthways and sliced crossways 12 mm (½ in) thick

1 tsp dried oregano

60 ml (2 fl oz) low-salt chicken or vegetable stock

Heat oil in a medium frying pan over medium-high heat. Add onion and sauté until it starts to soften, about 3 minutes. Stir in okra and sauté until it starts to soften, 3 minutes more.

Add tomatoes, oregano and stock. Cook, stirring often, until tomatoes are warmed through but not breaking down, 1–2 minutes. Serve warm.

To prepare: 20 minutes

To cook: 7 minutes

4 side-dish servings

swiss chard with lemon & anchovy

1 large bunch Swiss chard 375–440 g (12–14 oz)

3 Tbsp olive oil

180 ml (6 fl oz) low-salt vegetable or chicken stock

2 to 3 anchovy fillets, rinsed

2 Tbsp lemon juice

60 g (2 oz) chopped onion

90 g (3 oz) tinned chopped tomatoes or 2 plum tomatoes, seeded and chopped

Separate stems from chard leaves by cutting along both sides of centre vein. Stack leaves, roll up lengthways, and cut crossways into strips 2 cm (¾ in) wide. Trim off tough bottoms from stems and cut crossways into 12-mm (½-in) pieces.

To cook stems, heat 1 Tbsp oil in a frying pan over medium-high heat. Add stems and sauté for 5 minutes. Add 60 ml (2 fl oz) stock and cook until stems are tender and pan is almost dry, almost 4 minutes. Off heat, push stems to one side and mash anchovies in pan until creamy, using back of a wooden spoon, then add lemon juice and several grindings of pepper. Stir to incorporate. Arrange cooked stems on one side of a warmed serving platter. Rinse and dry pan.

To cook leaves, heat remaining 2 Tbsp oil in pan over medium-high heat. Add onion and sauté until golden, 6–7 minutes. Stir in sliced leaves in 3 or 4 batches, until wilted. Add tomatoes and remaining stock and cook, stirring occasionally, until chard is tender, about 10 minutes. Spoon leaves next to stems. Serve warm.

To prepare: 15 minutes

To cook: 25 minutes

4 side-dish servings

green figs with almond custard

2 Tbsp flaked almonds

250 ml (8 fl oz) semi-skimmed or whole milk

2 egg yolks

60 g (2 oz) sugar

2 or 3 drops almond extract

2 tsp butter

8 green figs, halved lengthways

125 ml (4 fl oz) unfiltered apple juice

Preheat oven to 180°C (350°F). Spread almonds in a single layer on a baking sheet. Toast for 3 minutes, stir and continue toasting until golden, 3–4 minutes more. Spread nuts at once on a plate to cool. Set aside.

Pour milk into a heavy saucepan and place over medium heat until small bubbles ring edges of pan. In a bowl, beat together egg yolks and sugar until creamy. Pour about 60 ml (2 fl oz) hot milk into egg mixture while whisking constantly. Return milk-egg mixture to pan and stir constantly over medium heat with a wooden spoon until mixture thickens and lightly coats the back of the spoon, about 2 minutes. Do not allow to boil. A cooking thermometer inserted into the custard should read 82°C (180°F). Remove from heat and stir in almond extract. Pour custard into a jug, place cling film directly on the surface to prevent skin from forming and refrigerate for 4 hours.

Just before serving, pour 60 ml (2 fl oz) custard onto the centre of each chilled dessert plate and set aside.

In a medium non-stick frying pan, heat butter over medium-high heat. Add figs, cut side down, and sauté until pale gold, about 1 minute. Add apple juice and boil until syrupy, about 3 minutes.

Arrange 4 fig halves on the custard on each plate. Decorate with almonds and serve.

To prepare: 10 minutes, plus 4 hours to chill

To cook: 8 minutes

4 dessert servings

cauliflower shallots mushrooms

WHITE AND TAN FRUITS AND VEGETABLES CONTAIN

dates turnips bananas tan figs

ANTIOXIDANTS FOR HEALING AND PROTECTION • HELP

tan pears parsnips white corn

MAINTAIN A HEALTHY CHOLESTEROL LEVEL • PROMOTE

potatoes jerusalem artichokes

HEART HEALTH • BOOST THE IMMUNE SYSTEM • SLOW

jicama kohlrabi white peaches

CHOLESTEROL ABSORPTION • WHITE AND TAN FRUITS

garlic white asparagus ginger

AND VEGETABLES OFFER ANTIOXIDANTS FOR HEALING

White & tan

Though subtle and understated in colour, this group of white and tan foods is a varied market basket, ranging from familiar root vegetables to earthy mushrooms to smooth and satisfying tropical fruits. Together they offer a wonderful panoply of enticing flavours and valuable vitamins, minerals and phytonutrients not available in more dramatically coloured produce.

Vegetables and fruits in this group include members of the healthful Allium genus—garlic, onions, leeks and shallots—along with mushrooms, white asparagus, sugar-sweet nectarines, pungent ginger and the ubiquitous breakfast-cereal topper, bananas.

We use alliums often for seasoning, but they are so beneficial that they deserve to be the centre of the dinner plate. An entrée of pork chops smothered under a heap of sautéed onions and apples touched with Calvados (page 63) proves that the alliums can star in a dish with delicious results.

Sicilian cooks enliven an already nutrient-rich cauliflower by sautéing it with a mix of capers, anchovies and nuts. Adding prawns turns this southern Italian side dish into an appealing main course (page 60).

Meaty mushrooms offer umami, the elusive "fifth taste" that lifts the flavour of all in the ingredients in a dish. Pan-searing them intensifies their taste (page 64), making them ideal for serving with fish, folded into an omelette, or alone.

SPRING	SUMMER	AUTUMN	WINTER
white asparagus	bananas & plantains	cauliflower	cauliflower
bananas & plantains	white corn	dates	celeriac
cauliflower	dates	fennel	dates
dates	white aubergine	tan figs	garlic
garlic	tan figs	Jerusalem artichokes	ginger
ginger	garlic	jicama	Jerusalem artichokes
jicama	ginger	kohlrabi	jicama
mushrooms	kohlrabi	mushrooms	onions
onions	mushrooms	onions	parsnips
parsnips	white nectarines	parsnips	tan pears
tan pears	onions	tan pears	potatoes
potatoes	white peaches	potatoes	shallots
shallots	tan pears	shallots	turnips
turnips	shallots	turnips	water chestnuts

white asparagus mimosa with browned butter

16 spears white asparagus

2 Tbsp butter

1 hard-boiled egg, whites finely chopped and yolk reserved

Peel lower halves of asparagus, paring away any woody parts.

Steam asparagus or blanch in boiling water for 4 minutes. Chill in ice water, drain and pat dry. (This step may be done up to 4 hours ahead.)

Melt butter in a large frying pan over medium-high heat. Add asparagus and sauté until butter starts to brown, 2–3 minutes. Divide asparagus among 4 warmed salad plates and spoon on butter from pan. Spoon chopped egg whites on top of asparagus. Press some egg yolk through a fine-mesh sieve over egg whites and serve.

To prepare: 20 minutes

To cook: 6 minutes

4 side-dish servings

potato galettes with smoked salmon

2 medium potatoes, about 375 g (12 oz) total, peeled

About 2 Tbsp rape seed or olive oil

90 g (3 oz) thinly sliced smoked salmon

1 Tbsp snipped fresh chives

1–2 Tbsp reduced-fat sour cream for garnish (optional)

Shred potatoes using largest holes of a box grater-shredder, holding them at a 45-degree angle to make long shreds. A small handful at a time, squeeze potatoes dry.

Heat 2 tsp oil in a medium frying pan over medium-high heat. Place 1 heaped Tbsp potato in pan for each galette, making 4 at a time. Using a pancake turner, firmly flatten potatoes into 7.5-cm (3-in) pancakes, repeatedly pressing to compact potatoes and pushing in loose edges so they do not burn. Work spatula under potatoes to prevent sticking. Keep pressing and lifting galettes until tops look translucent, about 3 minutes. Turn and cook, continuing to press and lift, until galettes are well browned, about 3 minutes more. While still hot, season to taste with salt and pepper. Wipe out pan.

Add oil by the teaspoon, as needed, and repeat, cooking galettes in 2 more batches. As pan gets hotter, potatoes will cook more quickly. Lower heat if necessary so galettes cook through in centre.

Serve galettes as they are cooked, topped with a 5-cm (2-in) square of smoked salmon and a sprinkle of chives. Dot with sour cream, if desired.

To prepare: 10 minutes

To cook: 20 minutes

4 starter servings (12 galettes)

sicilian prawns with cauliflower & almonds

90 g (3 oz) sultanas

375 g (12 oz) small prawns

about 375g (12 oz) 2.5 cm (1-in) cauliflower florets

2 Tbsp olive oil

185 g (6 oz) chopped onions

2 cloves garlic, finely chopped

185 g (6 oz) chopped plum tomatoes

4 anchovy fillets, rinsed

125 ml (4 fl oz) low-salt chicken stock

1 tsp dried basil

Pinch of red pepper flakes

30 g (1 oz) flaked almonds

In small bowl, cover sultanas with warm water and leave to stand until plump, about 20 minutes. Meanwhile, peel prawns. Drain sultanas and put sultanas and prawns aside.

Steam cauliflower until fork-tender, about 5 minutes. Drain and set aside.

Heat oil in a sauté pan over medium-high heat. Add onions and sauté until lightly browned, 8–10 minutes. Add garlic and tomatoes and cook, stirring occasionally, until tomatoes start to break down, 5 minutes. Add prawns and sauté until bright pink, about 3 minutes. Add anchovies, mashing them with back of a wooden spoon. Add cauliflower, sultanas, stock, basil and red pepper flakes. Lower heat to medium and cook until prawns are opaque in centre, about 3 minutes.

Remove from heat and stir in almonds. Serve on a warmed platter.

Note: Serve with steamed brown rice or cooked spaghetti.

To prepare: 25 minutes, plus 20 minutes to soak

To cook: 25 minutes

4 servings

potatoes with chorizo & parsley

750 g (1½ lb) large boiling potatoes, quartered

60 g (2 oz) peeled, thinly sliced hot or sweet dry chorizo (see Note)

30 g (1 oz) finely chopped red onion

60 ml (2 fl oz) dry white wine such as Chablis or Soave

2 Tbsp chopped fresh parsley

Boil potatoes until fork-tender, about 20 minutes. Drain and return potatoes to pot.

Heat a non-stick medium frying pan over medium-high heat. Add chorizo and sauté to render most of its fat, about 2 minutes. Pour off fat and continue cooking chorizo until lightly browned, 1–2 minutes more. Add onion and sauté for 1 minute. Add potatoes and wine and cook until most of liquid has evaporated, about 1 minute. Remove to a shallow serving bowl and toss with parsley. Serve warm.

Note: Use dry-cured chorizo for this dish, rather than the raw type, which can't be sliced. To peel chorizo, lightly run a sharp knife down its length. With your fingers, peel skin away from sausage, as if unwrapping it.

To prepare: 12 minutes

To cook: 25 minutes

4 side-dish servings

turkey fricassee with kohlrabi, pears & mushrooms

375 g (12 oz) boneless turkey breast

2 Tbsp rape seed oil

90 g (3 oz) chopped onion

2 Tbsp chopped shallot

45 g (1½ oz) plain flour

250 ml (8 fl oz) strong apple cider

90 g (3 oz) Dijon mustard

1 Tbsp ground coriander

1 pear, peeled, cored and diced

2 medium kohlrabi, peeled and diced

250 g (8 oz) white mushrooms, stemmed and quartered

Cut turkey into bite-sized pieces. Heat oil in a large sauté pan over medium-high heat. Add turkey and cook, stirring occasionally, until white on all sides, 3–4 minutes; lower heat if necessary to avoid scorching. Using slotted spoon, remove to a plate.

Return pan to medium-high heat, add onion and shallot, and sauté until translucent, about 4 minutes. Lower heat, stir in flour, and cook for 1 minute, stirring constantly. Add cider, which will splatter, and stir to combine with flour. Add mustard, coriander, pear, kohlrabi, mushrooms and turkey and stir well. Simmer, stirring occasionally, until turkey is opaque at the centre and vegetables and pear are tender, about 20 minutes.

Remove to a warmed serving bowl and serve at once.

Note: Serve accompanied with green beans and steamed brown rice.

To prepare: 20 minutes

To cook: 30 minutes

4 servings

pork chops smothered in onions & apples

2 Tbsp rape seed oil

500 g (1 lb) onions, halved and thinly sliced crossways

1 Golden Delicious apple, halved, cored and cut crossways into slices 6 mm (¼ in) thick

4 boneless pork chops, 125 g (4 oz) each

125 ml (4 fl oz) low-salt chicken stock

2 Tbsp Calvados

Heat 1 Tbsp oil in a medium sauté pan over medium-high heat. Add onions and sauté until wilted, about 5 minutes. Add apple and sauté for 2 minutes. Using slotted spoon, remove onions and apples to a plate.

Return pan to medium-high heat and add remaining 1 Tbsp oil. Season chops with ½ tsp salt and a few grindings of pepper. Sauté chops, turning once, until lightly browned on both sides, 4–5 minutes total. Spoon onion mixture over chops and cook until meat is barely pink in centre, 4–5 minutes. Remove onion and apples to warmed serving platter and arrange chops on top.

Add stock and Calvados to pan and stir to scrape up browned bits. Boil until liquid is reduced by half, about 4 minutes. Spoon sauce over meat and serve at once.

To prepare: 20 minutes

To cook: 22 minutes

4 servings

pan-seared mushrooms

Sauté thinly sliced white or cremini mushrooms in a dry skillet over medium-high heat until they release their liquid. Add minced garlic, salt, and pepper. Cook until mushrooms are dry and tender. Sprinkle with chopped parsley and serve.

garlic chips

Sauté thinly sliced garlic cloves in a generous amount of olive oil until pale gold on both sides, then drain on paper towels. The garlic turns crisp as it cools. Sprinkle on steamed vegetables and use to garnish soups.

hot & sour bok choy

Combine juice of ½ lime, 2 tsp sugar, red pepper flakes, and salt in a small bowl. Stir-fry 2.5-cm (1-in) slices of white part of mature bok choy in peanut oil for a minute. Add lime sauce and stir-fry for a minute more. Serve hot or warm.

plantain with jalapeño

Sauté a thinly sliced jalapeño chilli in coconut oil until fragrant. Set aside. Add a thinly sliced ripe plantain to pan. Cook until slices are golden on both sides. Drain on paper towels. Sprinkle jalapeño slices over plantain and serve at once.

mu shu pork

375 g (12 oz) lean pork such as boneless loin

Eight 20-cm (8-in) flour tortillas

2 Tbsp hoisin sauce

1 Tbsp low-salt soy sauce

1 Tbsp sherry

2 Tbsp low-salt chicken stock

2 tsp sugar

1 tsp Asian sesame oil

4 Tbsp peanut or rape seed oil

1 Tbsp finely chopped garlic

1 Tbsp finely chopped fresh ginger

1 carrot, cut into thin strips

1 stick celery, cut into thin strips

1 leek, white part only, cut into thin strips

125 g (4 oz) fresh shiitake mushrooms, stemmed and cut into thin strips

155 g (5 oz) tinned sliced water chestnuts, drained and cut into thin strips

Freeze meat for up to 1 hour to make it easier to slice. Thinly slice meat with the grain, then cut slices into thin strips. Set aside.

Preheat oven to 180°C (350°F). Wrap tortillas in foil and warm for 10 minutes in oven. Set aside.

In a small bowl, mix together hoisin and soy sauces, sherry, chicken stock, sugar and sesame oil. Set aside.

Heat oil in a wok over medium-high heat until almost smoking. Add pork and stir-fry until colour changes, then remove to a plate using a slotted spoon. Pour off all but 1 Tbsp peanut oil. Add garlic and ginger and stir-fry until fragrant, about 30 seconds. Add carrot, celery, leek, mushrooms and water chestnuts and stir-fry until vegetables are just tender, about 1½ minutes. Add hoisin sauce mixture and return meat to wok. Cook until opaque in centre, 1–2 minutes. Remove to a warmed platter and serve, accompanied with warmed tortillas.

To prepare: 35 minutes, plus 1 hour to freeze meat

To cook: 5 minutes

4 servings

turnips with peas & mushrooms

2 tsp grape seed or rape seed oil

4 small white turnips, about 500 g (1 lb) total, peeled and cut into 12-mm (½-in) wedges

160 ml (5 fl oz) low-salt chicken stock

155 g (5 oz) frozen peas

90 g (3 oz) pan-seared mushrooms (page 64), warmed

Heat oil in a large non-stick frying pan over medium-high heat. Add turnips and stir to coat with oil. Sauté for 1 minute; do not let turnips take on colour.

Add 125 ml (4 fl oz) stock. When it boils, lower heat and cook turnips for 3 minutes, then turn with tongs. When pan is almost dry, add remaining stock and cook until turnips are fork-tender, 3 minutes more. Add peas and heat through. Spoon vegetables into a wide, shallow serving bowl, top with mushrooms and serve.

To prepare: 15 minutes

To cook: 9 minutes

4 side-dish servings

chicken with caramelised shallots & wine

2 Tbsp butter

375 g (12 oz) large shallots, cut into slices 6-mm (¼ in) thick

2 tsp sugar

1 tsp freshly chopped fresh rosemary

4 skinless, boneless chicken breasts, 125–155 g (4–5 oz) each

125 ml (4 fl oz) light red wine such as a fruity Pinot Noir

125 ml (4 fl oz) low-salt chicken stock

1 tsp red wine vinegar

2 Tbsp fresh chervil leaves or chopped fresh parsley for garnish

Melt 1 Tbsp butter in a medium frying pan over medium-high heat. Add shallots and sauté until translucent, about 8 minutes. Stir in sugar and rosemary and cook until shallots are limp and gold, 8 minutes, lowering heat if needed to avoid burning. Remove shallots to a plate and wipe out pan with paper towels.

Pound each breast between 2 sheets of cling film, using a mallet or rolling pin, until 12 mm (½ in) thick. Heat 1 Tbsp butter in same pan over medium-high heat. Add chicken, season to taste with salt and pepper and sauté, turning often, until browned on both sides, about 12 minutes. Remove to a warmed serving platter and tent with foil.

Add shallots, wine, stock and vinegar to pan, bring to a boil, and stir to scrape up browned bits. Cook until liquid is reduced by half, about 4 minutes. Remove from heat. Spoon sauce over chicken. Garnish with chervil or parsley and serve at once.

To prepare: 20 minutes

To cook: 32 minutes

4 servings

white nectarines with tawny port

1 tsp butter

4 white nectarines, stoned and cut into slices 12 mm (½ in) thick

2 Tbsp sugar

Juice of ½ lemon (about 2 Tbsp)

4 Tbsp tawny port

8 *savoiardi* cookies or champagne biscuits

Melt butter in a medium non-stick frying pan over medium heat. Add nectarines and sauté until warm, about 1 minute. Sprinkle on sugar and add lemon juice. Sauté until sugar dissolves, about 30 seconds. Add port and cook until fruit just starts to soften, about 3 minutes. Remove nectarines to a wide, shallow bowl and leave to cool to room temperature.

Divide fruit among small bowls and serve with cookies.

To prepare: 5 minutes

To cook: 5 minutes

4 dessert servings

bananas with cinnamon-chocolate drizzle

125 g (4 oz) sugar

45 g (1½ oz) cocoa powder, sifted

¼ tsp ground cinnamon

60 g (2 oz) plain chocolate, chopped

1 Tbsp butter

2 Tbsp firmly packed light brown sugar

3 bananas, peeled and halved lengthways and crossways (see Note)

4 small scoops vanilla ice cream

Whisk sugar, cocoa and cinnamon together in a saucepan. Stir in 125 ml (4 fl oz) water and bring to a boil over medium-high heat, stirring with a wooden spoon. Lower heat and simmer for 1 minute more. Remove from heat and stir in chocolate until melted. Pour sauce into jug and set aside.

Melt butter in a frying pan over medium-high heat until it stops foaming. Sprinkle sugar over butter, covering bottom of pan evenly, and cook until it looks moist and dark, about 1 minute. Add bananas, cut side down, in a single layer and lower heat to medium. Cook until golden on bottom, about 2 minutes. Turn and cook for 1 minute more.

Arrange 3 banana quarters on each dessert plate. Drizzle 1 Tbsp cinnamon-chocolate sauce over each serving and top with a small scoop of vanilla ice cream. Serve at once.

Note: The bananas used for this dessert should be yellow and firm, with no brown spots, so that they hold together when cooked.

To prepare: 5 minutes

To cook: 10 minutes

4 dessert servings

grapefruit mangoes pineapples

YELLOW AND ORANGE FRUITS AND VEGETABLES HELP

apricots yellow pears pumpkins

PROMOTE HEART HEALTH • HELP REDUCE THE RISK OF

persimmons peaches kumquats

CERTAIN CANCERS • PROMOTE EYE HEALTH • CONTAIN

swedes golden beets carrots

ANTIOXIDANTS FOR HEALING AND PROTECTION • BOOST

yellow apples golden kiwifruits

THE IMMUNE SYSTEM • YELLOW AND ORANGE FRUITS

lemons navel oranges papayas

AND VEGETABLES OFFER ANTIOXIDANTS FOR HEALING

Yellow & orange

Corn, oranges, sweet potatoes, pumpkins, apples, pears, lemons—this chapter offers a basketful of vegetables and fruits that even picky eaters are happy to eat. These nutrient-rich members of the yellow and orange family get their eye-catching hues from carotenes, important antioxidants that give these fruits and vegetables their vibrant colour and a healthy load of vitamin A.

These antioxidants turn peppers, potatoes and berries usually associated with other colour groups a glowing gold or a sunny orange. Their colours—yellow and orange peppers, yellow-fleshed potatoes, pale gold raspberries—let you know they offer different benefits from their more familiarly coloured cousins.

Sautéing caramelises the natural sugars in the orange-fleshed sweet potatoes often called yams, giving a crust to creamy hash made with sweet potatoes, smoky ham and apples (page 87). Hard-shelled orange winter squashes and pumpkin can taste bland on their own, but coating thin slices with a dry spice rub adds the aromatic and hot flavours

of Indian curry (page 84). Swede turns irresistibly sweet when julienned and sautéed with golden beets until tender (page 84). And combining pineapple with preserved ginger illustrates how dry sautéing turns fresh fruit into an almost-instant dessert whose digestive benefits make it a perfect ending to a meal (page 82).

SPRING	SUMMER	AUTUMN	WINTER
carrots	apricots	yellow apples	yellow apples
grapefruit	yellow & orange peppers	dried apricots	dried apricots
golden kiwifruits	corn	golden beets	golden beets
kumquats	mangoes	yellow & orange peppers	carrots
lemons	orange-fleshed melon	lemons	grapefruit
mangoes	nectarines	navel & mandarin oranges	kumquats
navel & mandarin oranges	Valencia oranges	yellow pears	lemons
papayas	papayas	persimmons	navel & mandarin oranges
yellow-fleshed potatoes	passion fruit	yellow-fleshed potatoes	yellow pears
sweet potatoes	peaches	pumpkins	yellow-fleshed potatoes
orange-fleshed winter squash	pineapples	swedes	pumpkins
	golden raspberries	sweet potatoes	rutabagas
	yellow summer squash	orange-fleshed winter squash	sweet potatoes
	yellow tomatoes		orange-fleshed winter squash

spanish tortilla with golden potatoes

5 Tbsp olive oil

**750 g (1½ lb) potatoes, peeled and
cut into slices
3 mm (⅛ in) thick**

**1 leek, white and pale green part,
thinly sliced**

3 extra-large eggs

3 extra-large egg whites

Heat 2 Tbsp oil in a light-coloured, heavy frying pan over medium-high heat. Cover bottom of pan with one-quarter of potatoes, arranged in overlapping rings. Add one-third of leeks and 1 Tbsp oil. Repeat, finishing with potato layer. Cook for 5 minutes, working spatula under potatoes to prevent sticking. As potatoes on bottom brown, bring them to the top to let the others brown. Continue to stir occasionally for even cooking. When potatoes are almost soft, after about 20 minutes, turn them into a colander set over a bowl to drain. Reserve oil. Wipe out pan.

Beat eggs, egg whites and 1 tsp salt together in a large mixing bowl. Gently stir in potatoes and leeks.

Heat 2 Tbsp reserved oil in pan over medium-high heat. Add potato-egg mixture. Cook until set, about 5 minutes, lowering heat as needed to prevent scorching. Loosen tortilla by working spatula under and cook, shaking pan occasionally, until bottom is well browned, about 5 minutes more.

Slide tortilla onto a large plate. Invert pan over it. Holding plate and pan firmly in place, flip them, dropping uncooked side of tortilla into pan. Cook until browned on second side, about 5 minutes.

Slide tortilla onto a serving platter and leave to stand for at least 10 minutes, or until cool. Cut into wedges and serve.

To prepare: 25 minutes

To cook: 40 minutes

8 starter servings or
4 main-course servings

prawns with papaya & coconut

2 Tbsp unsweetened flaked coconut

1 Tbsp peanut oil

2 Tbsp finely chopped shallots

1 tsp grated fresh ginger

375 g (12 oz) medium prawns, peeled and deveined

155 g (5 oz) cubed papaya

75 g (2½ oz) cubed jicama

1 tsp curry powder

1 tin 470 g (15 oz) mandarin oranges, drained

10 g (⅓ oz) fresh coriander leaves for garnish

Toast coconut in a small, dry frying pan over medium heat, shaking pan constantly, until flakes are golden, about 4 minutes. Transfer at once to small bowl and set aside.

Heat oil in a medium non-stick frying pan over medium-high heat. Add shallots and ginger and sauté just until fragrant, about 30 seconds. Add prawns and cook, turning once, until bright pink on both sides, about 4 minutes total. Add papaya and jicama and sauté until prawns are browned in places on outside and opaque in centre, 3–4 minutes. Stir in curry powder and ¼ tsp pepper, and then oranges. Remove to a warmed serving platter, garnish with coconut and coriander and serve.

Note: Serve with steamed short-grain brown rice, if desired.

To prepare: 15 minutes

To cook: 12 minutes

4 servings

apricot-stuffed chicken breasts

12 dried apricot halves

6 stoned prunes

30 g (1 oz) dried apples

45 g (1½ oz) currants

⅛ tsp ground cardamom

2 cinnamon sticks

250 ml (8 fl oz) unfiltered apple juice, or as needed

125 ml (4 fl oz) brandy

60 ml (2 fl oz) brewed coffee

4 skinless, boneless chicken breasts, 185 g (6 oz) each

2 Tbsp butter

Combine apricots, prunes, apples, currants, cardamom, cinnamon, apple juice, brandy and coffee in a saucepan. Bring to the boil, cover, lower heat to a simmer and cook for 10 minutes. Set aside to soak until fruit is soft, about 30 minutes. Drain fruit, discarding cinnamon but reserving cooking liquid. If less than 1 cup, add more juice. Cool and coarsely chop apricots, prunes and apples.

Slit a deep pocket in each chicken breast, cutting in from thickest side to within 12 mm (½ in) on 3 sides. Pack each breast with dried fruit. Reserve leftover fruit for another use.

Melt butter in a medium sauté pan over medium heat. Brown breasts well on both sides, turning them every 2 minutes, about 8 minutes total. Add reserved liquid and simmer, turning chicken once, about 10 minutes. Remove chicken to a warmed platter. Boil liquid down to 80 ml (3 fl oz), 4 minutes. Strain, spoon over chicken and serve.

To prepare: 20 minutes, plus 30 minutes to soak

To cook: 32 minutes

4 servings

chicken with yellow peppers & passion fruit

500 g (1 lb) skinless, boneless chicken breasts

2 yellow peppers

1 small green pepper

2 Tbsp grape seed oil

1 onion, chopped

1 large clove garlic, finely chopped

1 tsp dried oregano

60 ml (2 fl oz) fresh passion fruit juice (see Note)

1 Tbsp champagne vinegar

Steamed brown, basmati or jasmine rice for serving

Slice chicken into 12-mm (½-in) strips. Season to taste with salt and pepper. Stem, seed and slice peppers lengthways into 12-mm (½-in) strips; stem, seed and cut green pepper into 3-mm (⅛-in) strips.

In a large non-stick frying pan, heat 1 Tbsp oil over medium-high heat. Cook chicken until white on all sides, 4 minutes total. Remove to a plate.

Heat remaining 1 Tbsp oil in pan. Sauté onion, yellow and green peppers and garlic until onion is translucent, 4 minutes. Return chicken and any accumulated juices to pan. Add oregano and cook until chicken is white in centre, about 3 minutes. Stir in passion fruit juice and vinegar and cook 1 minute more. Serve with rice.

Note: To make passion fruit juice, scrape pulp and seeds from 2 fresh passion fruits into a blender or mini-food processor. Whirl with 125ml (4fl oz) water and strain through a fine-mesh sieve.

To prepare: 15 minutes

To cook: 13 minutes

4 servings

---

stuffed squash blossoms

250 g (8 oz) part-skimmed ricotta cheese

60 g (2 oz/) finely diced mozzarella cheese

30 g (1 oz) freshly grated Parmigiano-Reggiano cheese

2 Tbsp chopped fresh parsley

12 large squash blossoms

125 g (4 oz) plain flour

125 ml (4 fl oz) olive oil

Drain ricotta in a strainer lined with muslin for 2 hours in refrigerator. Combine ricotta, mozzarella and Parmesan cheeses with parsley, ½ tsp salt and several grindings of pepper in a bowl.

Rinse blossoms, checking them for insects and remove bitter stamens. Gently spoon 1 generous Tbsp cheese mixture into each blossom and press ends closed, twisting them together.

In a small bowl, whisk flour with cold water, starting with 80 ml (3 fl oz), until it has consistency of double cream. Leave batter to rest for 30 minutes.

Heat oil in a small frying pan over medium-high heat. Holding each end, dip 3 blossoms in batter and let excess drip back into bowl. Add blossoms to hot oil and pan-fry, turning once with tongs, until golden and crisp, 3–4 minutes. Using a slotted spoon, remove blossoms, shake and place on a paper towel to drain. Season to taste with salt and serve cooked blossoms at once while frying remaining ones.

To prepare: 25 minutes, plus 2 ½ hours to stand

To cook: 12 minutes

Makes 4 side-dish servings (12 blossoms)

peppered yellow pears with honey

Sauté quartered cored pears in butter and lemon juice, turning to coat. When warmed through, transfer to plates and add 3 Tbsp lavender honey and coarse black pepper to the pan. Spoon syrup on pears and serve with fresh goat's cheese.

pineapple with preserved ginger

Sear fresh, sliced pineapple rings in a dry non-stick frying pan until golden on both sides. Place on plates and sprinkle generously with brown sugar. Top with finely chopped preserved ginger in a syrup or rinsed crystallised ginger.

sautéed summer squash with corn

Sauté thinly sliced rounds of yellow summer squash and fresh corn kernels in butter. Add a splash of chicken broth and chopped spring onions. Cook, stirring often, until pan is almost dry. Garnish with fresh basil threads.

savoury sautéed persimmons

Melt butter in a large pan over medium heat. Add zest and juice of ½ orange, 1 Tbsp Worcestershire sauce and thin crossways slices of persimmon. Cook, stirring, until sauce thickens slightly. Serve with pork or chicken.

swede & golden beetroot with pomegranate seeds

1 medium swede
375 g (12 oz), peeled and halved lengthways

1 large golden beetroot, 250 g (8 oz), peeled and halved lengthways

1 Tbsp olive oil

1 tsp sugar

180 ml (6 fl oz) low-salt chicken or vegetable stock

125 g (4 oz) pomegranate seeds

Cut swede halves crossways into slices 3 mm (⅛ in) thick. Stack 3 or 4 slices at a time and cut into 3 mm (⅛ in) matchsticks. Cut beetroots in the same fashion.

Heat oil in a medium sauté pan over medium-high heat. Add swede and sauté for 3 minutes. Add beetroots and sauté for 3 minutes more, lowering heat to prevent vegetables from browning.

When vegetables deepen in colour, add sugar and stock and cook until vegetables are fork-tender, about 5 minutes more. Using a slotted spoon, remove vegetables to a warmed serving bowl. Sprinkle on pomegranate seeds, season to taste with salt and pepper, toss and serve.

To prepare: 25 minutes

To cook: 12 minutes

4 to 6 side-dish servings

indian-spiced squash with cashews

½ tsp ground cumin

½ tsp sweet paprika

¼ tsp ground turmeric

Pinch of cayenne pepper

375 g (12 oz) squash or pumpkin, halved, seeded, peeled, and cut into slices 6 mm (¼ in) thick (see Notes)

1 Tbsp ghee or clarified butter (see Notes)

2 Tbsp unsweetened shredded coconut

2 Tbsp roasted cashews, coarsely chopped

Combine spices and ½ tsp salt in a small bowl. Arrange squash on a plate and sprinkle with spice mixture, coating slices on both sides. Leave to stand for 30 minutes.

Heat ghee in a large non-stick frying pan over medium-high heat. Add squash to pan in a single layer. Cook, turning once, until squash is fork-tender, about 6 minutes total. Using tongs, remove to a serving platter. Wipe out pan with paper towels.

Return pan to medium-high heat and add coconut and cashews. Toast, stirring, until coconut is golden and nuts are warm, 1–2 minutes. Sprinkle them over the squash, and then sprinkle with ½ tsp salt. Serve warm or at room temperature.

Notes: Ghee, the clarified butter used in Indian cooking, is sold in natural food stores and Indian markets. For more on clarified butter, see page 96. To aid in peeling squash, microwave it for 1 minute to soften skin.

To prepare: 15 minutes, plus 30 minutes to stand

To cook: 8 minutes

6 side-dish servings

ham & sweet potato hash

2 medium orange-fleshed sweet potatoes (yams), 375 g (12 oz) total, peeled and cut into slices 2 cm (¾ in) thick

4 tsp rape seed oil

155 g (5 oz) finely chopped red onion

75 g (2½ oz) finely diced Granny Smith apple

90 g (3 oz) sliced Black Forest or Westphalian ham, chopped

2 tsp fresh thyme leaves or 1 tsp dried thyme

¼ tsp sweet paprika

1 Tbsp white vinegar

6 eggs

Steam sweet potato slices until centre just resists light pressure, about 8 minutes. Leave to cool to room temperature or refrigerate for up to 24 hours.

Heat 2 tsp oil in a medium non-stick frying pan over medium-high heat. Add onion and apple and sauté over medium-high heat until onion is browned, about 10 minutes. Remove to a mixing bowl and wipe out pan.

Dice sweet potatoes and add them to bowl with onion and apple. Stir in ham, thyme and paprika, using a fork to mash potatoes coarsely.

Heat 2 tsp oil in same pan over medium-high heat. Add hash mixture in 90 g (3 oz) mounds, flattening them with a spatula into patties 2 cm (¾ in) thick. Brown well on both sides, turning after 4–5 minutes. If they break apart, pat back into shape. Place the patties on plates.

While hash cooks, poach eggs. Fill a deep sauté pan with cold water. Add vinegar and 1 tsp salt and set pan over medium heat. When water begins to simmer, break eggs, one at a time, into a cup and slip each one gently into the water. Cook for 1 minute, slide spatula under eggs to avoid sticking, and poach to desired doneness, 3–5 minutes. Using a slotted spoon, remove eggs and place on hash. Serve at once.

To prepare: 15 minutes

To cook: 30 minutes

6 servings

butternut squash & pears with rosemary

375 g (12 oz) bottom rounded part of butternut squash

1 Tbsp grape seed or rape seed oil

1 pear, halved, cored and cut into slices 6 mm (¼ in) thick

1 Tbsp finely chopped fresh rosemary

Pinch of cayenne pepper

125 ml (4 fl oz) apple juice

Peel squash, halve lengthways, remove seeds and strings and cut lengthways into thin slices.

Heat oil in a frying pan over medium-high heat. Add squash and season with 1 tsp salt. Sauté until squash begins to soften, about 5 minutes, lowering heat if needed so squash does not colour. Add pear, rosemary, cayenne and apple juice and cook until liquid evaporates and squash is tender, 6–8 minutes. Serve hot, warm, or at room temperature.

To prepare: 20 minutes

To cook: 12 minutes

4 side-dish servings

peach shortcake

Shortcakes

155 g (15 oz) plus 2 Tbsp plain flour

2 Tbsp plus ½ tsp sugar

1 Tbsp baking powder

1 tsp ground cinnamon

¼ tsp salt

5 Tbsp cold butter, cut into small pieces

125 ml (4 fl oz) low-fat or whole buttermilk

½ tsp pure vanilla extract

2 Tbsp unsalted butter

1 bag (500 g / 1 lb) peaches, peeled and sliced

80 ml (3 fl oz) orange juice

90 g (3 oz) maple syrup

Sweetened whipped cream for serving

For Shortcakes: Preheat oven to 200°C (400°F). Have ready an ungreased baking sheet.

In a bowl, whisk together flour, 2 Tbsp sugar, baking powder, cinnamon and salt until well blended. Cut in 5 Tbsp butter until mixture resembles coarse crumbs. Add buttermilk and vanilla and gently toss with fork or rubber spatula until flour is just moistened and ingredients are blended.

Turn dough out onto lightly floured work surface. Gently press dough into a thick 10-cm (4-in) square. Trim edges even with large sharp knife, then cut into 4 equal squares.

Place squares on baking sheet, spacing them well apart. Sprinkle remaining ½ tsp sugar over tops. Bake until puffed and golden, 15–18 minutes. Remove to wire rack to cool completely.

Meanwhile, melt 2 Tbsp butter in a large non-stick frying pan over medium-high heat. Add peaches in a single layer and cook, turning once with tongs, until warmed through, about 2 minutes total. Add orange juice and simmer until peaches are fork-tender, about 4 minutes more. Add maple syrup and simmer until peaches are glazed and some syrup remains in pan, 1–2 minutes. Set aside to cool to lukewarm.

To serve, split or cut shortcakes in half horizontally and place bottom halves, cut side up, on dessert plates. Spoon some of the peaches, including syrup, over each half and top with a dollop of whipped cream. Top with remaining shortcake halves, cut side down. Serve at once.

To prepare: 25 minutes

To cook: 25 minutes

4 dessert servings

rhubarb cranberries red onions

RED FRUITS AND VEGETABLES PROVIDE ANTIOXIDANTS

beets radishes ruby grapefruit

FOR PROTECTION AND HEALING • PROMOTE HEART

cherries watermelon red plums

HEALTH • PROMOTE URINARY TRACT HEALTH • HELP

tomatoes red pears raspberries

REDUCE THE RISK OF CERTAIN CANCERS • IMPROVE

pomegranates red peppers

MEMORY FUNCTION • RED FRUITS AND VEGETABLES

radicchio strawberries quinces

OFFER ANTIOXIDANTS FOR PROTECTION AND HEALING

Red

Many red fruits and vegetables—sweet peppers and tomatoes, red onions and hot chillis, red apples and red grapes—work well in sautés and stir-fries, while others—cherries and cranberries—compliment sautéed meats, fish and poultry. All of them are good for you, and some, including strawberries and raspberries, boast the highest concentration of antioxidants.

Red fruits are frequently served with game, but they complement ordinary poultry, meat and fish as well. The chopped cranberry-orange relish widely enjoyed at American Thanksgiving meals can be enhanced with red onion and apple and warmed in the pan used for sautéing turkey tenderloin for a delicious combination any time of the year

(page 99). For a flavour and colour revelation, try spaghetti cooked in red wine in place of water and served topped with sautéed red pepper, onion and broccoli (page 95). Sautéed trout sauced with red wine and grapes is a bold update of a French classic that provides all the health benefits found in red grapes (page 96).

The traditional duck with orange sauce gains a new colour profile when thinly sliced sautéed duck breast is served on a bed of watercress leaves and drizzled with a simple reduction of blood orange juice, a fat-free sauce whose flavour balances bittersweet caramelised sugar with the mildly acidic, berry-nuanced scarlet red juice (page 99).

SPRING	SUMMER	AUTUMN	WINTER
beetroots	cherries	red apples	red apples
redcurrants	red peppers	beetroots	beetroots
pink & red grapefruit	red chillis	red peppers	cranberries
red onions	redcurrants	red chillis	pink & red grapefruit
blood oranges	red onions	cranberries	red grapes
red potatoes	red plums	red grapes	blood oranges
radicchio	radishes	red pears	pomegranates
radishes	raspberries	red plums	red potatoes
rhubarb	strawberries	pomegranates	quinces
strawberries	tomatoes	quinces	radicchio
	watermelon	red potatoes	radishes
		raspberries	

warm tomato & olive bruschetta

1 Tbsp olive oil

370 g (12 oz) chopped fresh plum tomatoes (4 medium)

3 Tbsp green olives, chopped lengthways

2 tsp chopped fresh oregano or ½ tsp dried oregano

1 Tbsp capers, rinsed and chopped

4 slices rustic Italian wholemeal bread

2 cloves garlic, halved

Heat oil in a frying pan over medium-high heat. Add tomatoes, olives and oregano and sauté until tomatoes start to soften, about 1 minute. Remove from heat and stir in capers and a few grindings of black pepper. Set aside.

Grill or toast bread. Rub warm bread generously on one side with cut side of the garlic halves. Top with warm tomato mixture and serve.

To prepare: 10 minutes

To cook: 5 minutes

4 starter servings

red wine spaghetti with red pepper & onion

375 g (12 oz) whole-wheat spaghetti

1 bottle (750 ml) medium- to full-bodied red wine such as Merlot or Zinfandel

2 Tbsp olive oil

2 Tbsp chopped garlic

250 g (8 oz) 2.5-cm (1-in) broccoli florets

1 large red pepper, seeded and sliced

1 red onion, diced

125 g (4 oz) shiitake mushrooms, stemmed and quartered

30 g (1 oz) crumbled feta cheese

Cook pasta in salted boiling water for about 8 minutes. It will still be quite hard. Drain and return pasta to pot. Add wine and cook until pasta is just under al dente, 2–3 minutes. Drain spaghetti in colander set over a bowl, reserving the wine.

Meanwhile, heat oil in a medium sauté pan over medium-high heat. Add garlic and sauté for 1 minute. Add broccoli, pepper, onion and mushrooms and cook until broccoli is tender-crisp, about 5 minutes. Add pasta and reserved wine and cook, stirring a few times, until three-quarters of the liquid has evaporated. Divide among warmed wide, shallow bowls, sprinkle with cheese and serve at once.

To prepare: 10 minutes

To cook: 20 minutes

4 servings

sautéed trout with red grape sauce

500 ml (16 fl oz) light, fruity red wine, such as a Beaujolais

60 g (2 oz) finely chopped carrots

45 g (1½ oz) finely chopped celery

30 g (1 oz) finely chopped onion

2 sprigs fresh thyme

1 small bay leaf

⅛ tsp whole peppercorns

4 skin-on trout fillets, 185 g (6 oz) each

45 g (1½ oz) plain flour

2 Tbsp clarified butter or olive oil (see Note)

125 g (4 oz) halved seedless red grapes

2 tsp cold butter, diced

Boil wine, carrot, celery, onion, thyme, bay leaf and peppercorns in a saucepan until reduced to 125 ml (4 fl oz), about 12 minutes. Strain through a fine-mesh sieve into a bowl, pressing on vegetables with the back of a wooden spoon. Discard vegetables and set wine aside for up to 4 hours.

Pat fish dry with paper towels. Season to taste with salt and pepper. Dredge fillets in flour and shake off excess. Heat clarified butter in a frying pan just large enough to hold fish. While shaking pan, add trout, skin side up, and continue shaking for 1 minute to prevent sticking. Cook until fish is golden brown, 2–3 minutes. Using a wide spatula, turn trout and cook, again shaking pan for 30 seconds to prevent sticking. Cook until fish is just opaque when tested in the centre at thickest point, 1–2 minutes. Place fillets on a warmed plate and tent loosely with foil. Wash out the pan and dry thoroughly.

Add reduced wine and grapes to pan over medium heat and simmer until grapes are heated through, 1 minute. Off heat, swirl in cold butter. Place fillets on warmed plates. Spoon sauce over fish and serve.

Note: Clarified butter, which is butter with the milk solids removed, does not burn at the high temperatures used for sautéing. It can be purchased by the jar in speciality-food shops. To prepare your own, slowly melt unsalted butter in saucepan over medium-low heat. When white solids sink to bottom, pour off clear yellow liquid through a fine-mesh strainer into a heatproof container. Cover tightly and refrigerate up to 1 month.

To prepare: 15 minutes

To cook: 20 minutes

4 servings

duck with blood orange sauce

90 g (3 oz) sugar

310 ml (10 fl oz) blood orange juice (from about 6 oranges), plus 2 blood oranges, peeled and sectioned

4 duck breast halves, 185 g (6 oz) each, fat trimmed

1 bunch watercress, stemmed

3 Tbsp pomegranate seeds for garnish (optional)

Place sugar and 1 Tbsp water in a heavy saucepan, tilting pan to wet sugar. Boil over medium-high heat, swirling occasionally, until mixture turns a golden caramel color, 3 minutes. Off heat, pour in orange juice; be careful, as it will splatter. Return to heat and boil until frothy bubbles rise above syrupy liquid, 10–13 minutes. Set aside.

Place duck, skin side down, in a large non-stick frying pan over medium heat. Sprinkle with salt and pepper. Cook until skin is light gold, about 8 minutes, then pour off fat. Lower heat and cook until skin is dark brown, 10 minutes more. Turn and cook for 4 minutes for medium-rare, or 5 minutes for medium. Remove to a plate and leave to rest for 5 minutes.

Divide watercress among warmed plates. Slice the duck thinly, with the grain. Arrange slices along edge of watercress, overlapping. Fan 5 or 6 orange sections next to duck. Spoon 2 Tbsp sauce over duck. Sprinkle with pomegranate seeds, if using, and serve.

To prepare: 25 minutes

To cook: 35 minutes

4 servings

turkey tenderloin with cranberry compote

250 g (8 oz) fresh or frozen cranberries

1 apple, peeled, cored and chopped

1 small red onion, diced

1 strip orange zest, 2.5 cm x 7.5 cm (1 in x 3 ins)

1 Tbsp rape seed oil

500 g (1 lb) turkey tenderloin, cut lengthways into 2 cm (¾ in) strips

125 ml (4 fl oz) low-salt chicken stock

1 Tbsp sugar

½ tsp stuffing seasoning

Pulse cranberries, apple, onion and orange zest in a food processor until coarsely chopped. Set aside.

Heat oil in a medium non-stick frying pan over medium-high heat. Add turkey and sauté until browned on all sides and opaque in centre, about 8 minutes total. Remove to a plate and tent with foil.

Add stock to pan and stir, scraping up browned bits. Add cranberry mixture, sugar and stuffing seasoning to pan. Cook over medium heat, stirring occasionally, until mixture resembles thick applesauce, about 10 minutes. Spoon warm compote beside tenderloin and serve.

Note: Serve with mashed roasted sweet potatoes and steamed green beans. Refrigerate leftover compote for up to 1 week. Substitute ½ tsp ground thyme, ¼ tsp ground ginger and pinch of ground pepper for stuffing seasoning.

To prepare: 15 minutes

To cook: 20 minutes

4 servings

prosciutto grapes

Wrap whole seedless red grapes with thin strips of prosciutto, overlapping it and pressing firmly. Sauté grapes in a lightly oiled pan, shaking constantly, until grapes and prosciutto are golden. Season with pepper. Serve warm, on cocktail sticks.

warm ruby grapefruit salad

Sauté thinly sliced red onion and jalapeño in a pan coated with cooking oil spray for 1 minute. Gently mix in sliced avocado and ruby grapefruit sections until warmed. Serve on tender lettuce, sprinkled with fresh coriander.

hungarian red peppers

Sauté red pepper and red onion strips in some rape seed oil until soft, about 10 minutes. Mix in 2 tsp sweet paprika. Off heat, stir in 125 g (4 oz) sour cream. Serve warm with sautéed pork, chicken or tofu.

herbed cherry tomatoes

Heat cherry tomatoes in a pan with olive oil, shaking to toss for a minute. Add chopped rosemary and garlic, salt and pepper. Continue rolling the tomatoes in the pan until wilted and soft to the touch, 2–4 minutes. Scoop into a serving bowl.

rib steak with red wine pan sauce & bronze onions

1 tsp olive oil

4 boneless rib steaks, each 2 cm (¾ in) thick, well-trimmed

2 Tbsp demiglace mixed with 125 ml (4 fl oz) water, or 125ml (4 fl oz) low-salt beef stock

180 ml (6 fl oz) full-bodied red wine such as Zinfandel

¼ tsp crushed peppercorns

1 tsp cold butter, diced

1 red onion, cut crossways into slices 6 mm (¼ in) thick

Cooking oil spray for greasing

Heat oil in a large frying pan over medium-high heat. Season steak to taste with salt and pepper. Add steaks and brown on first side, about 4 minutes. Using tongs, turn and cook on second side until browned and cooked to desired degree of doneness: 3 minutes for rare, 4 minutes for medium, 5 minutes for well done. Transfer steaks to warmed dinner plates and keep warm.

Add demiglace mixture or beef stock to pan and boil until reduced by half, about 4 minutes. Add wine and peppercorns and boil until reduced to 125 ml (4 fl oz), 4–5 minutes. Off heat, swirl in butter. Spoon sauce over meat. Set aside.

Lightly coat a medium cast-iron frying pan with cooking oil spray. Once the pan is hot sear onion rings, turning once with tongs, until they look bronze, about 4 minutes total. Divide the onion rings evenly over the steaks and serve at once.

To prepare: 5 minutes

To cook: 15–25 minutes

4 servings

sautéed radicchio with pancetta

1 large head radicchio, about 315 g (10 oz)

30 g (1 oz) pancetta, chopped

1 Tbsp red wine vinegar

Cut radicchio lengthways into 12-mm (½-in) wedges. Trim away most of white core, leaving just enough to hold leaves together. Add pancetta to a cold medium frying pan, set over medium heat, and sauté until fat is rendered and pancetta is golden, about 5 minutes. Remove from pan with a slotted spoon and set aside.

Add radicchio to pan and cook in pancetta fat until leaves are mostly wilted and white parts are lightly golden, about 5 minutes. Add vinegar and stir to coat radicchio.

Remove radicchio to warmed serving plate and sprinkle with reserved pancetta. Serve at once.

To prepare: 8 minutes

To cook: 10 minutes

4 starter or side-dish servings

pork tenderloin with sour cherry sauce

45 g (1½ oz) dried sour cherries

125 ml (4 fl oz) unsweetened cherry juice

1 Tbsp rape seed oil

375–500 g (12 oz-1 lb) pork tenderloin, cut into slices 12 mm (½ in) thick

60 ml (2 fl oz) ruby port

30 g (1 oz) finely chopped red onion

¼ tsp ground coriander

30 g (1 oz) plain chocolate, finely chopped

Soak cherries in juice until plumped, about 20 minutes. Drain, reserving the soaking liquid.

Heat oil in a medium sauté pan over medium-high heat. Season pork to taste with salt and pepper. Add pork and cook, turning once and reducing heat so meat does not brown, about 3 minutes total. Arrange meat in 2 rows on warmed serving platter, overlapping the slices. Tent with foil and set aside.

Add reserved cherry juice, plumped cherries, port, onion and coriander to pan. Bring to a boil, scraping up any browned bits, and cook until liquid is reduced by one-third, 4–5 minutes. Off heat, stir in chocolate until sauce thickens slightly, about 1 minute.

Spoon sauce over each row of pork medallions and serve.

To prepare: 10 minutes, plus 20 minutes to plump

To cook: 9 minutes

4 servings

red-hot hash browns

375 g (12 oz) walnut-sized red new potatoes

1 Tbsp rape seed oil

60 g (2 oz) finely chopped onion

60 g (2 oz) finely chopped red pepper

½ tsp sweet paprika

1 fresh red chilli, thinly sliced

Place potatoes in a saucepan of cold water and bring to the boil. Boil until fork-tender, about 12 minutes. Drain and cool in cold water or leave to stand until cooled to room temperature. Using a sharp knife, halve potatoes.

Heat oil over medium-high heat in a frying pan large enough to hold potatoes in a single layer. Add onions and peppers and sauté until onion is translucent, about 4 minutes. Stir in paprika. Add potatoes, cut side down, and cook until browned and crusty on first side, 4–5 minutes. Add chilli and 1 tsp salt. Cook, stirring, until some of the onions are deeply browned, about 1 minute more. Serve potatoes in a shallow bowl.

Note: If you prefer a milder dish, omit the chilli, or seed the chilli and use less. Leftover boiled or roasted potatoes, cut into 4-cm (1½ in) pieces, can also be used in this recipe.

To prepare: 10 minutes

To cook: 25 minutes

4 side-dish servings

strawberries
in red wine

500 ml (16 fl oz) top quality
vanilla ice cream

1 Tbsp butter

375 g (12 oz) fresh strawberries,
hulled, larger ones
halved lengthways

2 Tbsp Demerara sugar or light
brown sugar

125 ml (4 fl oz) fruity but structured
red wine, such as a light Cabernet
Sauvignon or Merlot

4 mint sprigs (optional)

Scoop ice cream into four 60-g (2 oz) balls and arrange on a plate. Freeze until ice cream is hard, about 1 hour. (Cover with foil if holding ice cream longer.) Save remaining ice cream for another use.

Melt butter in medium frying pan over medium-high heat. Sauté berries for 1 minute. Add sugar, wine and 7 or 8 grindings of pepper. When liquid boils, reduce heat and simmer fruit for 1 minute more, until sugar is dissolved and smaller berries are soft on the outside but still firm in the centre. Let berries stand for 15 minutes to cool.

While berries cool, remove ice cream from freezer and leave to stand at room temperature to soften slightly. It should still be firm, so that it melts slowly into the warm fruit rather than all at once.

Divide strawberries and wine among 4 dessert bowls or large wine goblets. Top each with a scoop of ice cream and decorate with mint, if using. Serve at once.

To prepare: 12 minutes, plus 1 hour to freeze

To cook: 2 minutes, plus 15 minutes to cool

4 dessert servings

toasted madeira cake
with cherries

250 ml (8 fl oz) unsweetened
cherry juice

90 g (3 oz) sugar

60 ml (2 fl oz) Cointreau or
Triple Sec liqueur

2 strips lemon zest, each
5 cm x 2.5 cm (2 ins x 1 in)

½ tsp coriander seeds

¼ tsp peppercorns

500 g (1 lb) sweet cherries, stoned

4 slices madeira cake, each 2.5 cm
(1 in) thick

Combine cherry juice, sugar, liqueur, lemon zest, coriander and peppercorns in a saucepan. Bring to the boil, lower heat and simmer for 5 minutes. Remove from heat, cover and steep for 1 hour. Strain, discarding spices. Return liquid to pan, add cherries and simmer until cherries are tender. If not using at once, cover and set aside for up to 8 hours at room temperature, then reheat before serving.

Heat a non-stick frying pan over medium heat. Add cake slices and dry-sauté until browned on both sides, turning once and wiping out pan as needed when cake sticks to surface, 30–60 seconds total.

To serve, place cake slices on dessert plates. Spoon warm fruit and syrup over cake.

To prepare: 5 minutes, plus 1 hour to steep

To cook: 6 minutes

4 dessert servings

almonds kidney beans peanuts

WHOLE GRAINS, LEGUMES, SEEDS AND NUTS PROMOTE

pecans chestnuts bulgur wheat

ARTERY AND HEART HEALTH • HELP REDUCE THE RISK

flaxseed sesame seeds polenta

OF DIABETES • REDUCE HIGH BLOOD PRESSURE • OFFER

pumpkin seeds cashews quinoa

ANTIOXIDANTS FOR PROTECTION AND HEALING • HELP

kasha macadamia nuts walnuts

REDUCE THE RISK OF STROKE • MAY REDUCE THE RISK

hazelnuts oats couscous millet

OF CANCERS OF THE BREAST, PROSTATE AND COLON

Brown

Foods in the brown group are the foundation of healthy eating. Many are whole foods—grains, legumes, nuts, seeds—rich in the vitamins, minerals, fibre and unsaturated oils essential for well-being. Their actual colours range from pale cashews and beige oats to golden polenta, brown rice and black beans. But whatever their hue, they are indispensable to a beneficial dietary regimen.

Whole grains are usually dense and chewy, but many of them can be dry-sautéed to lighten their texture. For example, toasting quinoa in a dry pan before adding liquid yields a light pilaf to pair with chicken breasts and gingery mango-yoghurt sauce (page 120). You can also combine grains with sautéed vegetables, fruits and nuts, such as couscous with dried fruits, a simple pairing of flavours and textures (page 113).

Legumes are a great source of the dietary fibre we need every day, and cooks pressed for time will be happy to know that tinned beans or quick-cooking lentils are a good way to fulfill this daily requirement. Small brown lentils mixed with sautéed celery, shallot and diced serrano ham and tossed with a sherry vinaigrette make a satisfying main course (page 123).

Nuts and seeds also provide fibre along with heart-protecting fats. Try cashews in a stir-fry (page 117), or candied walnuts as a sweet, crunchy topping for a maple-flavoured panna cotta (page 124).

GRAINS	LEGUMES	SEEDS	NUTS
amaranth	black beans	flaxseed	almonds
barley	cannellini beans	pumpkin seeds	Brazil nuts
bulgur wheat	chickpeas	sesame seeds	cashews
couscous	cranberry (borlotti) beans	sunflower seeds	chestnuts
kasha (buckwheat groats)	kidney beans		hazelnuts
millet	butter beans		macadamia nuts
oats	soybeans		pecans
polenta	black-eyed peas		pine nuts
quinoa	split peas		pistachio nuts
brown rice	lentils		walnuts
whole wheat	peanuts		
	tofu		

ginger couscous
with dried fruit

1 Tbsp olive oil

30 g (1 oz) pine nuts

½ tsp ground ginger

125 g (4 oz) instant
semolina couscous

45 g (1½ oz) currants

45 g (1½ oz) chopped
dried peach (about 1 large half)

45 g (1½ oz) chopped
dried pear (about 1 large half)

2 Tbsp chopped crystallised ginger

Heat 2 tsp oil in a frying pan over medium heat. Add pine nuts and sauté, stirring constantly, until golden, 1–2 minutes. Using a slotted spoon, remove nuts to a plate. Lightly wipe out pan.

Add 330 ml (11 fl oz) water, ground ginger, 1 tsp salt and remaining 1 tsp oil to pan. Bring to the boil over medium-high heat. Stir in couscous, currants, peaches, pears and crystallised ginger. Remove from heat, cover and leave to stand for 5 minutes. Fluff couscous with a fork, stir in pine nuts and serve hot or warm.

Note: Serve with stir-fried dark greens or grilled chicken.

To prepare: 5 minutes

To cook: 7 minutes

4 servings

tamarind prawns
with peanuts

2 Tbsp peanut oil

45 g (1½ oz) unsalted peanuts

125 g (4 oz) chopped shallots

2 Tbsp finely chopped garlic

2 Tbsp finely chopped fresh ginger

2 Tbsp finely chopped lemongrass,
white part only (see Notes)

1–2 fresh red chillis, thinly sliced
(optional)

375 g (12 oz) medium-sized prawns,
peeled and deveined

60 ml (2 fl oz) tamarind water
(see Notes)

2 Tbsp Asian fish sauce

1 tsp sugar

280 g (9 oz) diced
fresh pineapple

Have ready a small plate lined with paper towels. Heat oil in a wok over medium-high heat until almost smoking. Add peanuts and stir-fry briefly, until just taking on colour. Remove wok from heat and, using a slotted spoon, remove peanuts to paper towels to drain. Reserve oil.

Return wok to burner and heat oil again until almost smoking. Add shallots, garlic, ginger, lemongrass and chillis, if using, and stir-fry until fragrant, about 30 seconds. Add prawns and stir-fry until bright pink, about 2 minutes.

Add tamarind water, fish sauce, sugar and ⅛ tsp pepper and stir-fry until prawns are opaque in centre, 1–2 minutes. Stir in pineapple and heat through. Serve at once, garnished with fried peanuts.

Notes: For lemongrass, cut off and discard green top from stalk. Peel off dry outer layers from white base. Using a sharp knife, cut this base crossways into very thin slices. For tamarind water, dissolve 1 Tbsp tamarind concentrate (available at Indian and Southeast Asian groceries) in 3 Tbsp warm water. Serve this dish over short-grain brown rice.

To prepare: 20 minutes

To cook: 5 minutes

4 servings

turkey with red mole

Mole

1–2 dried chillis, seeded

2 Tbsp raisins

Boiling water as needed

2 cloves garlic

1 small onion, quartered

3 large tomatillos, husked and rinsed

2 Tbsp flaked almonds

1 Tbsp unsweetened cocoa powder

⅛ tsp ground cloves

80 ml (3 fl oz) low-salt chicken stock

**One 15-cm (6-in) corn tortilla,
torn into 2.5-cm (1-in) pieces**

1 Tbsp rape seed oil

**3 or 4 turkey tenderloins,
about 500 g (1 lb)**

160 ml (5 fl oz) low-salt chicken stock

**Steamed spinach for serving
(see Note)**

For Mole: Heat a cast-iron frying pan over medium-high heat. One at a time, rinse chillis and roast in dry pan, pressing with a heatproof spatula and turning them until softened and fragrant, about 2 minutes. Wearing latex gloves, tear chillis into 2.5-cm (1-in) pieces and place in a heatproof bowl. Add raisins and boiling water to cover. Leave to soak until chillis are soft, about 20 minutes. Drain chillis and raisins and place in a blender.

Heat a dry sauté pan over medium-high heat, add garlic and onion, and pan-roast, turning often with tongs, until browned and blistered on all sides, 4–5 minutes. Remove to a cutting board. Add tomatillos to pan and dry-roast in same manner until browned and blistered on all sides, about 5 minutes. Remove to cutting board. Coarsely chop vegetables, transfer to a blender. Allow pan to cool and wipe out.

Add almonds, cocoa powder, 1 tsp salt, ¼ tsp pepper, cloves and 80 ml (3 fl oz) chicken stock to blender. Blend to make a coarse purée. Add tortilla and blend until purée is smooth.

Heat oil in same cast-iron frying pan over medium-high heat. Season turkey to taste with salt and pepper. Cook turkey until lightly browned on all sides, about 6 minutes total. Add mole and 160 ml (5 fl oz) chicken stock. Bring to the boil, lower heat, and simmer until turkey is opaque in centre at its thickest point, about 15 minutes.

Remove turkey from pan and leave to rest on a cutting board for 5 minutes. Slice turkey and arrange on a warmed serving platter, overlapping slices. Spoon mole over the top. Serve at once.

Note: Serve with steamed spinach, kale or steamed brown rice.

*To prepare: 30 minutes,
plus 20 minutes to soak*

To cook: 35 minutes

4 servings

cashew chicken stir-fry

1 medium head iceberg lettuce, quartered

2 Tbsp hoisin sauce

1 Tbsp low-sodium soy sauce

1 tsp rice vinegar

60 ml (2 fl oz) low-salt chicken stock

1 Tbsp cornflour

¼ tsp Asian sesame oil

2 Tbsp peanut oil

375 g (12 oz) skinless, boneless chicken breasts, cut into 12-mm (½-in) cubes

1 Tbsp finely chopped garlic

4 spring onions, white and tender green parts, cut into slices 12 mm (½ in) thick

1 medium green pepper, seeded and diced

1 large red pepper, seeded and diced

1 fresh green chilli, thinly sliced

60 g (2 oz) coarsely chopped raw cashews

With your fingers, separate 3 layers from each of the lettuce quarters, making 4 lettuce cups. Place lettuce cups on a plate, cover with moist paper towels and refrigerate.

In a small bowl, mix together hoisin sauce, soy sauce, vinegar, chicken stock and cornflour. Stir in sesame oil and set aside.

In a wok, heat peanut oil over medium-high heat until almost smoking. Add chicken and stir-fry until it changes colour, 1–2 minutes. Using a slotted spoon, remove chicken to a plate. Add garlic, spring onions, peppers and chilli and stir-fry until tender-crisp, about 2 minutes. Return chicken to wok and add nuts. Stir seasoning sauce again, add to wok, and stir-fry until chicken is cooked through, 2–3 minutes.

Divide stir-fry among chilled lettuce cups and serve at once.

To prepare: 30 minutes

To cook: 7 minutes

4 servings

white beans with tomato & bacon

Fry 2 slices bacon until crisp, then sauté a chopped small onion in the bacon fat. Stir in rinsed and drained tinned white beans, chopped plum tomato, chopped rosemary and pepper. When heated through, crumble the bacon over.

popped amaranth

Add 3 Tbsp amaranth seeds to a dry, hot wok, vigorously shaking pan until they stop popping (some will brown and not pop). In a bowl, combine amaranth with a few drops grape seed oil, chilli powder and sea salt, mixing with your fingers.

crunchy breakfast topping

Sauté 1 Tbsp *each* raw sunflower and sesame seeds in a small sauté pan until fragrant and lightly coloured. Combine with 1 Tbsp *each* toasted wheat germ, ground flaxseed and brown sugar. Sprinkle on yogurt or over cereal.

peanut sambal

Combine 2 Tbsp *each* coconut milk, peanut butter and lime juice with 1 Tbsp fish sauce and red pepper flakes. Stir-fry cubed firm tofu with chopped garlic and ginger in oil until aromatic. Add sauce and stir-fry until thick. Season with salt.

mango chicken
with toasted quinoa

125 g (4 oz) quinoa, rinsed and drained

3 Tbsp low-fat or whole plain yoghurt

1 tsp grated fresh ginger

1 tsp honey

1 Tbsp lemon juice

315 g (10 oz) diced mango

125 g (4 oz) diced seeded cucumber

4 skinless, boneless chicken breasts, 185 g (6 oz) each

1 Tbsp rape seed oil

Toast wet quinoa in a dry non-stick sauté pan over medium heat, stirring with a wooden spatula, until grains are dry, 2–3 minutes. Raise heat to medium-high and stir constantly until grains start popping. When quinoa is lightly browned, about 6 minutes, remove from heat and pour in 500 ml (16 fl oz) water; be careful, as it will splatter. Cover and simmer over medium-low heat until tender, about 15 minutes.

Meanwhile, whisk together yoghurt, ginger, honey and ¼ tsp salt in a mixing bowl. Stir in lemon juice, mango and cucumber. Set aside.

Pound breasts to an even thickness between 2 sheets of cling film, using a mallet or rolling pin. Rub chicken on both sides with ½ tsp salt and ¼ tsp pepper. Heat oil in a large non-stick frying pan over medium-high heat. Add chicken and sauté until browned, 3–4 minutes per side. Reduce heat and cook until chicken is opaque in centre, about 3 minutes more. To serve, fluff quinoa with a fork and divide among warmed dinner plates. Top with chicken and mango mixture.

To prepare: 20 minutes

To cook: 35 minutes

4 servings

kasha with walnuts & pasta

2 Tbsp rape seed oil

125 g (4 oz) kasha (see Note)

375 ml (12 fl oz) low-salt vegetable broth

90 g (3 oz) bow-tie pasta

185 g (6 oz) diced onion

45 g (1½ oz) chopped walnuts

Heat 1 Tbsp oil in a saucepan. Add kasha and cook, stirring constantly, until grains darken, about 3 minutes. Pour in broth; be careful, as it will splatter. Lower heat, cover and cook until kasha is soft, about 10 minutes. Off heat, leave to stand, covered, for 5 minutes. Fluff grains with a fork, season to taste with salt and pepper and cover to keep warm.

While kasha cooks, cook pasta in salted boiling water until al dente, about 12 minutes. Drain and set aside.

Meanwhile, heat remaining 1 Tbsp oil in a medium frying pan over medium-high heat. Add onion and sauté until golden, about 8 minutes. Mix in cooked kasha, pasta and ⅛ tsp pepper and stir until kasha is heated through. Sprinkle with walnuts and serve.

Note: Kasha is roasted buckwheat groats.

To prepare: 5 minutes

To cook: 25 minutes

4 servings

black bean & white corn salad

2 tsp rape seed oil

75 g (2½ oz) chopped red pepper

90 g (3 oz) chopped red onion

220 g (7 oz) drained cooked or tinned black beans

185 g (6 oz) fresh or frozen corn kernels

1 tsp chilli powder

2 Tbsp lime juice

Romaine (cos) lettuce leaves for serving (optional)

15 g (½ oz) chopped fresh coriander

Heat oil in a medium frying pan over medium-high heat. Add pepper and onion and sauté until juice from pepper moistens bottom of pan, about 3 minutes.

Stir in beans, corn and chilli powder. Cook until beans and corn are heated through, about 3 minutes. Corn and peppers will be tender-crisp. Remove pan from heat and stir in lime juice. Toss well and season to taste with salt and pepper.

Line a platter with lettuce leaves, if using, and spoon beans and corn on top. Or spoon beans and corn into a warmed serving bowl. Garnish with coriander and serve.

To prepare: 10 minutes

To cook: 6 minutes

4 side-dish servings

lentils with shallots & serrano ham

155 g (5 oz) brown lentils, rinsed

1 Tbsp olive oil

125 g (4 oz) finely chopped celery

45 g (½ oz) finely chopped shallots

2 Tbsp sherry vinegar

60 g (2 oz) serrano ham, finely diced

lettuce leaves for serving

Combine lentils and 750 ml (24 fl oz) water in a deep saucepan and place over medium-high heat until liquid boils. Reduce heat to maintain a simmer, cover and cook until tender, about 35 minutes. Drain lentils in a colander set over a mixing bowl; there will be about 440 g (14 oz). Remove lentils to a bowl, reserving 60 ml (2 fl oz) cooking liquid.

Heat oil in a medium frying pan over medium-high heat. Add celery and shallots and sauté until golden, about 8 minutes. Add contents of pan to lentils. Add vinegar and reserved lentil-cooking liquid to pan, bring to the boil and reduce liquid by half, 3 minutes. Add hot liquid to lentils and stir in ham. Season to taste with salt and pepper.

Line a serving bowl or platter with lettuce leaves, mound lentils on top, and serve.

To prepare: 30 minutes

To cook: 45 minutes

4 servings

maple panna cotta
with candied walnuts

Cooking oil spray for greasing

500 ml (16 fl oz) skimmed milk

4 tsp unflavoured gelatin

105 g (3½ oz) maple sugar

250 ml (8 fl oz) double cream

125 g (4 oz) coarsely chopped walnuts

2 Tbsp sugar

Pinch of Chinese five-spice powder

250 ml (8 fl oz) peanut or rape seed oil

Coat six 180-ml (6-fl oz) individual custard cups or ramekins with cooking oil spray and set on a small baking sheet.

Pour 125 ml (4 fl oz) milk into a saucepan and sprinkle on the gelatin. Allow gelatin to soften, about 5 minutes. Add remaining 375 ml (12 fl oz) milk and maple sugar and cook over medium heat, stirring constantly, until sugar and gelatin are dissolved, about 5 minutes. Do not allow liquid to boil. Pour mixture into a mixing bowl. Set bowl into a larger bowl filled with ice water. Whisk until mixture starts to thicken and registers 18°C (65°F) on an instant-read thermometer, about 10 minutes. Gently stir in cream. Divide mixture evenly among prepared dishes, cover with cling film, and refrigerate until firm, at least 3 hours.

Cover another baking sheet with heavy-duty foil and a third sheet with paper towels. Set both aside. Bring 1 litre (32 fl oz) water to the boil in a saucepan. Add nuts. When water returns to the boil, drain nuts and place in a bowl. Sprinkle hot nuts with sugar and spice and mix with a rubber spatula until sugar completely dissolves and nuts look shiny.

Heat oil in a wok over medium-high heat until it registers 190°C (375°F) on a sugar thermometer. Carefully add the nuts. Let them cook for 30 seconds, then stir-fry gently until evenly browned. Quickly remove nuts using a slotted spoon and drain on foil-lined pan. When cool, remove to paper towel-lined pan and blot off excess oil with more towels. Break nuts into pieces.

About 30 minutes before serving, remove ramekins from refrigerator and dip carefully in hot water to loosen custards. Invert and unmould custards onto dessert plates. Just before serving, sprinkle each panna cotta with walnuts. Place extra nuts in a little dish and set on the table for diners to nibble.

Note: Candied walnuts will keep for 2 days in an airtight container at room temperature.

To prepare: 25 minutes, plus 3 hours to chill

To cook: 15 minutes

6 dessert servings

Nutrients at work

Humans need more than forty nutrients to support life. Many foods are good sources of these various nutrients, but no single food provides everything. Eating a variety of foods, preferably in their whole form, is the best way to get all the nutrients your body needs. Some nutrients require others for optimal absorption, but excessive amounts may result in health problems.

Until recently, nutritionists believed that the distribution of carbohydrates, protein and fat in a healthy diet to be 55 percent of calories from carbohydrates, 15 percent of calories from protein, and 30 percent of calories from fat. As we have learned more about individual health needs and differences in our metabolism, we have become more flexible in determining what will constitute a well-balanced diet. The table below shows macronutrient ranges recommended in September 2002 by the Institute of Medicine, part of the U.S. National Academies. These ranges are more likely to accommodate everyone's health needs. To help you evaluate and balance your diet as you prepare the recipes in this book, turn to pages 130–33 for nutritional analyses of each recipe.

Nutrition experts have also determined guidelines for vitamins and minerals. For more information, see pages 128–29.

CARBOHYDRATES, PROTEIN, AND FATS

NUTRIENTS AND FOOD SOURCES	FUNCTIONS	RECOMMENDED % OF DAILY CALORIES AND GUIDANCE
Carbohydrates COMPLEX CARBOHYDRATES • Grains, breads, cereals, pastas • Dried beans and peas, lentils • Starchy vegetables (potatoes, corn, green peas)	• Main source of energy for the body • Particularly important for the brain and nervous system • Fibre aids normal digestion	45–65% • Favour complex carbohydrates, especially legumes, vegetables and whole grains (brown rice; whole-grain bread, pasta and cereal). • Many foods high in complex carbohydrates are also good fibre sources. Among the best are bran cereals, tinned and dried beans, dried fruit and rolled oats. Recommended daily intake of fibre for adults under age 50 is 25 g for women and 38 g for men. For women over age 50, intake is 21 g; for men, 30 g.
SIMPLE CARBOHYDRATES • Naturally occurring sugars in fruits, vegetables and milk • Added refined sugars in soft drinks, sweets, baked goods, jams and jellies, etc.	• Provide energy	• Fruit and vegetables have naturally occurring sugars but also have vitamins, minerals and phytochemicals. Refined sugar, on the other hand, has little to offer in the way of nutrition, so limit your intake to get the most from your daily calories.

Source: Institute of Medicine. Dietary Reference Intakes for Energy, Carbohydrates, Fibre, Fat, Protein, and Amino Acids (Macronutrients).

CARBOHYDRATES, PROTEIN AND FATS

NUTRIENTS AND FOOD SOURCES	FUNCTIONS	RECOMMENDED % OF DAILY CALORIES AND GUIDANCE
Protein • Foods from animal sources • Dried beans and peas, nuts • Grain products	• Builds and repairs cells • Regulates body processes by providing components for enzymes, hormones, fluid balance, nerve transmission	10–35% • Choose lean sources such as dried beans, fish, poultry, lean cuts of meat, soy and low-fat dairy products most of the time. • Egg yolks are rich in many nutrients but also high in cholesterol; limit to 5 per week.
Fats All fats are mixtures of saturated and unsaturated (polyunsaturated and monounsaturated) types. Polyunsaturated and especially monounsaturated types are more desirable because they promote cardiovascular health.	• Supply essential fatty acids needed for various body processes and to build cell membranes, particularly of the brain and nervous system • Transport certain vitamins	20–35% • Experts disagree about the ideal amount of total fat in the diet. Some say more is fine if it is heart-healthy fat; others recommend limiting total fat. Virtually all experts agree that saturated fat, trans fats, and cholesterol, all of which can raise "bad" (LDL) cholesterol, should be limited.
PRIMARILY SATURATED • Foods from animal sources (meat fat, butter, cheese, cream) • Coconut, palm, palm kernel oils	• Raises blood levels of "bad" (LDL) cholesterol	• Limit saturated fat.
PRIMARILY POLYUNSATURATED (PUFA) • Omega-3 fatty acids: herring, salmon, mackerel, lake trout, sardines, sword-fish, nuts, flaxseed, rape seed oil, soy-bean oil, tofu • Omega-6: vegetable oils such as corn, soybean, and safflower	• Reduces inflammation; influences blood clotting and blood vessel activity to improve blood flow	• Eat fish at least twice a week. • Substitute PUFA for saturated fat or trans fat when possible.
PRIMARILY MONOUNSATURATED (MUFA) Olive oil, rape seed oil, sesame oil, avocados, almonds, chicken fat	• Raises blood levels of "good" (HDL) cholesterol	• Substitute MUFA for saturated fat or trans fat when possible.
DIETARY CHOLESTEROL Foods from animal sources (egg yolks, organ meats, cheese, fish roe, meat)	• A structural component of cell membranes and some hormones	• The body makes cholesterol, and some foods contain dietary cholesterol.
TRANS FAT Processed foods, purchased baked goods, margarine and shortening	• Raises blood levels of "bad" (LDL) cholesterol	• Limit trans fat.

FAT-SOLUBLE VITAMINS AND FOOD SOURCES	FUNCTIONS	DAILY RECOMMENDED INTAKES FOR ADULTS*
Vitamin A Dairy products, deep yellow-orange fruits and vegetables, dark green leafy vegetables, liver, fish, fortified milk, cheese, butter	• Promotes growth and healthy skin and hair • Helps build strong bones and teeth • Works as an antioxidant that may reduce the risk of some cancers and other diseases • Helps night vision • Increases immunity	700 mcg for women 900 mcg for men
Vitamin D Fortified milk, salmon, sardines, herring, butter, liver, fortified cereals, fortified margarine	• Builds bones and teeth • Enhances calcium and phosphorus absorption and regulates blood levels of these nutrients	5–10 mcg
Vitamin E Nuts and seeds, vegetable and seed oils (corn, soybean, sunflower), whole-grain breads and cereals, dark green leafy vegetables, dried beans and peas	• Helps form red blood cells • Improves immunity • Prevents oxidation of "bad" LDL cholesterol • Works as an antioxidant that may reduce the risk of some cancers	15 mg
Vitamin K Dark green leafy vegetables, carrots, asparagus, cauliflower, cabbage, liver, wheat bran, wheat germ, eggs	• Needed for normal blood clotting • Promotes protein synthesis for bone, plasma and organs	90 mcg for women 120 mcg for men

WATER-SOLUBLE VITAMINS

B vitamins Grain products, dried beans and peas, dark green leafy vegetables, dairy products, meat, poultry, fish, eggs, organ meats, milk, brewer's yeast, wheat germ, seeds	• Helps the body use carbohydrates (biotin, B_{12}, niacin, pantothenic acid) • Regulate metabolism of cells and energy production (niacin, pantothenic acid) • Keep the nerves and muscles healthy (thiamin) • Protect against spinal birth defects (folate) • Protect against heart disease (B_6, folate)	• B_6: 1.3–1.5 mg • B_{12}: 2.4 mcg • Biotin: 30 mcg • Niacin: 14 mg niacin equivalents for women; 16 mg for men • Pantothenic acid: 5 mg • Riboflavin: 1.1 mg for women; 1.3 mg for men • Thiamin: 1.1 mg for women; 1.2 mg for men • Folate: 400 mcg
Vitamin C Many fruits and vegetables, especially citrus fruits, broccoli, tomatoes, green peppers, melons, strawberries, potatoes, papayas	• Helps build body tissues • Fights infection and helps heal wounds • Helps body absorb iron and folate • Helps keep gums healthy • Works as an antioxidant	75 mg for women 90 mg for men

Sources: Institute of Medicine reports, 1999–2001

*mcg=micrograms; mg=milligrams

MINERALS ** AND FOOD SOURCES	FUNCTIONS	DAILY RECOMMENDED INTAKES FOR ADULTS *
Calcium Dairy products (especially hard cheese, yoghurt and milk), fortified juices, sardines and tinned fish eaten with bones, shellfish, tofu (if processed with calcium), dark green leafy vegetables	• Helps build bones and teeth and keep them strong • Helps heart, muscles and nerves work properly	1,000–1,200 mg
Iron Meat, fish, shellfish, egg yolks, dark green leafy vegetables, dried beans and peas, grain products, dried fruits	• Helps red blood cells carry oxygen • Component of enzymes • Strengthens immune system	18 mg for women 8 mg for men
Magnesium Nuts and seeds, whole-grain products, dark green leafy vegetables, dried beans and peas	• Helps build bones and teeth • Helps nerves and muscles work properly • Necessary for DNA and RNA • Necessary for carbohydrate metabolism	310–320 mg for women 400–420 mg for men
Phosphorus Seeds and nuts, meat, poultry, fish, dried beans and peas, dairy products, whole-grain products, eggs, brewer's yeast	• Helps build strong bones and teeth • Has many metabolic functions • Helps body get energy from food	700 mg
Potassium Fruit, vegetables, dried beans and peas, meat, poultry, fish, dairy products, whole grains	• Helps body maintain water and mineral balance • Regulates heartbeat and blood pressure	2,000 mg suggested; no official recommended intake
Selenium Mushrooms, seafood, chicken, organ meats, brown rice, wholemeal bread, peanuts, onions	• Works as an antioxidant with vitamin E to protect cells from damage • Boosts immune function	55 mg
Zinc Oysters, meat, poultry, fish, soybeans, nuts, whole grains, wheat germ	• Helps body metabolise proteins, carbohydrates and alcohol • Helps wounds heal • Needed for growth, immune response and reproduction	8 mg for women 11 mg for men

** The following minerals are generally sufficient in the diet when the minerals listed above are present: chloride, chromium, copper, fluoride, iodine, manganese, molybdenum, sodium, and sulfur. For information on functions and food sources, consult a nutrition book.

Nutritional values

The recipes in this book have been analysed for significant nutrients to help you evaluate your diet and balance your meals throughout the day. Using these calculations, along with the other information in this book, you can create meals that have the optimal balance of nutrients. Having the following nutritional values at your fingertips will help you plan more healthy meals.

Keep in mind that the calculations reflect nutrients per serving unless otherwise noted. Not included in the calculations are optional ingredients or those added to taste, or that are suggested as an alternative or used as a substitution in the recipe, recipe note, or variation. For recipes that yield a range of servings, the calculations are for the middle of that range. Many recipes call for a specific amount of salt and also suggest seasoning food to taste; however, if you are on a low-sodium diet, it is prudent to omit salt. If you have particular concerns about any nutrient needs, consult your doctor.

The numbers for all nutritional values have been rounded using the guidelines required for reporting nutrient levels in the "Nutrition Facts" panel on food labels.

The best way to acquire the nutrients your body needs is through food. However, a balanced multivitamin-mineral supplement or a fortified cereal that does not exceed 100 percent of the daily need for any nutrient is a safe addition to your diet.

WHAT COUNTS AS A SERVING?	HOW MANY SERVINGS DO YOU NEED EACH DAY?		
	For a 1,600-calorie-per-day diet *(children 2–6, sedentary women, some older adults)*	For a 2,200-calorie-per-day diet *(children over 6, teen girls, active women, sedentary men)*	For a 2,800-calorie-per-day diet *(teen boys, active men)*
Fruit Group 1 medium whole fruit such as apple, orange, banana or pear 60–90 g (2–3 oz) chopped, cooked or tinned fruit 90 g (3 oz) dried fruit 180 ml (6 fl oz) fruit juice	2	3	4
Vegetable Group 30 g (1 oz) raw, leafy vegetables 60–90 g (2–3 oz) other vegetables, cooked or raw 180 ml (6 fl oz) vegetable juice	3	4	5
Bread, Cereal, Rice and Pasta Group 1 slice of bread 180 g (6 oz) ready-to-eat cereal 80 g (2.5 oz) cooked cereal, rice, pasta	6	9	11

Adapted from USDA Dietary Guidelines (2005).

Purple & blue		CALORIES	PROTEIN/ GM	CARBS/ GM	TOT. FAT/ GM	SAT. FAT/ GM	CHOL/ MG	FIBRE/ GM	SODIUM/ MG
p.23	Purple asparagus with orange vinaigrette	39	2	7	1	0	0	1	2
p.23	Purple carrots glazed with red wine	89	1	11	2	1	5	3	81
p.24	Salmon with wild blueberry & rhubarb sauce	238	24	18	8	1	53	2	59
p.27	Stir-fried pork with black plums	198	17	22	5	1	51	3	63
p.27	Duck with purple cabbage, blackberries & port	319	25	16	16	3	128	3	92
p.30	Sichuan beef with aubergine	372	23	33	16	4	28	4	333
p.33	Wild rice with purple pepper & pecans	209	4	22	13	2	0	3	4
p.33	Pan-fried blue potatoes with sage	85	1	10	5	1	0	1	2
p.34	Blackberry crêpes	452	10	75	12	7	83	4	258
p.34	Pomegranate-glazed figs	168	2	24	9	5	23	3	13

Green		CALORIES	PROTEIN/ GM	CARBS/ GM	TOT. FAT/ GM	SAT. FAT/ GM	CHOL/ MG	FIBRE/ GM	SODIUM/ MG
p.41	Stir-fried chicken with broccoli & mushrooms	275	18	29	10	2	31	4	455
p.41	Dry-fried long beans	85	2	8	6	0	0	3	9
p.42	Chicken breasts stuffed with goat's cheese & rocket	391	44	14	16	5	111	3	262
p.45	Stir-fried calamari & pea shoots	375	24	39	17	3	198	5	244
p.45	Chicken breasts with tomatillo sauce	180	24	5	6	1	63	1	76
p.48	Fettuccine with broad beans, artichokes & asparagus	528	24	82	15	3	6	19	228
p.48	Lemon sole with peas	270	35	12	8	4	97	3	143
p.51	Okra with yellow plum tomatoes	66	2	8	4	1	0	3	15
p.51	Swiss chard with lemon & anchovy	134	3	7	11	2	2	2	304
p.52	Green figs with almond custard	224	5	39	6	3	110	3	35

White & tan		CALORIES	PROTEIN/ GM	CARBS/ GM	TOT. FAT/ GM	SAT. FAT/ GM	CHOL/ MG	FIBRE/ GM	SODIUM/ MG
p.59	White asparagus mimosa with browned butter	82	3	3	7	4	68	1	18
p.59	Potato galettes with smoked salmon	156	5	16	8	1	5	1	429
p.60	Sicilian prawns with cauliflower & almonds	277	20	26	12	2	129	5	328
p.60	Potatoes with chorizo & parsley	189	6	29	4	2	9	3	143
p.63	Turkey fricassee with kohlrabi, pears, & mushrooms	293	25	28	10	1	34	4	599
p.63	Pork chops smothered in onions & apples	296	25	15	14	3	67	2	359
p.66	Mu shu pork	593	29	68	22	5	54	6	990
p.69	Turnips with peas & mushrooms	86	5	12	3	0	0	5	174
p.69	Chicken with caramelised shallots & wine	261	25	16	8	4	78	1	81
p.70	White nectarines with tawny port	198	4	36	3	1	83	3	34
p.70	Bananas with cinnamon-chocolate drizzle	372	5	70	11	6	12	5	19

Yellow & orange		CALORIES	PROTEIN/ GM	CARBS/ GM	TOT. FAT/ GM	SAT. FAT/ GM	CHOL/ MG	FIBRE/ GM	SODIUM/ MG
p.77	Spanish tortilla with golden potatoes	190	6	17	11	2	90	1	348
p.78	Prawns with papaya & coconut	184	15	18	6	2	126	2	149
p.78	Apricot-stuffed chicken breasts	484	40	44	10	5	116	4	192
p.81	Chicken with yellow peppers & passion fruit	345	29	33	11	2	67	3	64
p.81	Stuffed squash blossoms	368	15	21	24	8	32	1	287
p.84	Swede & golden beetroots with pomegranate seeds	96	3	14	4	1	0	3	80
p.84	Indian-spiced squash with cashews	57	1	4	5	2	5	1	189
p.87	Ham & sweet potato hash	178	10	14	9	2	219	2	258
p.87	Butternut squash & pears with rosemary	98	1	17	4	0	0	3	4
p.88	Peach shortcake	496	6	59	26	16	76	3	482

Red		CALORIES	PROTEIN/ GM	CARBS/ GM	TOT. FAT/ GM	SAT. FAT/ GM	CHOL/ MG	FIBRE/ GM	SODIUM/ MG
p.95	Warm tomato & olive bruschetta	139	5	19	5	1	0	5	346
p.95	Red wine spaghetti with red pepper & onion	581	17	78	10	2	6	14	117
p.96	Sautéed trout with red grape sauce	419	36	14	14	6	122	0	54
p.99	Duck with blood orange sauce	482	44	33	19	5	231	2	448
p.99	Turkey tenderloin with cranberry compote	212	27	16	5	1	56	3	78
p.102	Rib steak with red wine pan sauce & bronze onions	574	30	7	43	17	118	0	387
p.102	Sautéed radicchio with pancetta	47	2	3	3	1	5	1	74
p.105	Pork tenderloin with sour cherry sauce	239	19	17	10	3	55	1	49
p.105	Red-hot hash browns	111	2	19	4	0	0	2	5
p.106	Strawberries in red wine	246	3	25	13	8	72	2	51
p.106	Toasted madeira cake with cherries	325	3	61	6	3	63	2	123

Brown		CALORIES	PROTEIN/ GM	CARBS/ GM	TOT. FAT/ GM	SAT. FAT/ GM	CHOL/ MG	FIBRE/ GM	SODIUM/ MG
p.113	Ginger couscous with dried fruit	244	5	38	10	1	0	5	586
p.113	Tamarind prawns with peanuts	412	24	45	15	2	129	4	834
p.114	Turkey with red mole	361	33	40	9	1	56	5	106
p.117	Cashew chicken stir-fry	334	24	20	18	4	51	3	324
p.120	Mango chicken with toasted quinoa	389	39	37	10	2	94	4	97
p.120	Kasha with walnuts & pasta	292	7	37	15	1	0	5	178
p.123	Black bean & white corn salad	132	6	22	3	0	0	6	23
p.123	Lentils with shallots & serrano ham	181	13	24	5	1	6	9	202
p.124	Maple panna cotta with candied walnuts	392	7	22	32	12	61	1	53

Glossary

almonds: See Nuts.

amaranth: This ancient grain is particularly high in protein and fibre and is also rich in many minerals, including iron, phosphorus, copper, magnesium and manganese.

ancho chillis: See Chillis.

apples: The major portion of the apple's nutrition is in its skin, which contains the flavonoid quercetin, an antioxidant that fights viruses and allergies and is thought to be an anticarcinogenic. However, apple flesh is an important source of pectin, a fibre that lowers cholesterol.

apricots: The apricot's colour is due to the pigments beta-carotene and lycopene, which promote eye health and heart health, lower the risk of some cancers and strengthen the immune system. Apricots are also high in vitamin C, potassium, and fibre.

artichokes: The artichoke's fleshy heart provides a complex of heart-healthy phyto-chemicals, including cynarin; it also contains chlorophyll and beta-carotene and provides a wide range of vitamins and minerals.

Asian chilli sauce or paste: Used as a seasoning or condiment to add heat in Chinese and Southeast Asian dishes, this seasoning is made from fresh or dried red chillis. You can find it at Asian groceries and speciality-food stores.

Asian dark sesame oil: This dark sesame oil is made from toasted or roasted sesame seeds. Heat harms its flavour, so add it after cooking and use it to give sauces and dressings rich, aromatic flavour. It is sold in the ethnic sections of well-stocked supermarkets and in Asian and speciality-food stores. Seek out Japanese brands for the best quality.

asparagus: This vegetable is one of the best sources of folate, a B vitamin that helps fight heart disease. It is also rich in phytochemicals, especially the flavonoid rutin and a host of vitamins and minerals. It comes in green, purple and white hues.

aubergines: The purple skin of the familiar globe aubergine is rich in heart- and brain-healthy anthocyanins, while its flesh contains saponins, antioxidants that help to lower cholesterol levels. Other varieties may be slightly smaller and have lavender, white, rose, green or variegated skin.

bananas: Bananas are high in potassium, which balances sodium and helps regulate blood pressure, and may reduce arterial plaque formation. Potassium also helps to prevent strokes by lowering platelet activity and reducing blood clots. Bananas are also high in vitamins C and B$_6$, and contain a kind of fibre that is believed to protect against colon cancer.

basil: Traditionally used in kitchens throughout the Mediterranean and in Southeast Asia, basil is one of the world's best-loved herbs and is a source of green phytonutrients. Although related to mint, basil tastes faintly of anise and cloves. Italian cooks use it in pesto and often pair it with tomatoes. In Thailand and Vietnam, basil is often combined with fresh mint for seasoning stir-fries, curries and salads.

beans, black: Also called turtle beans, these have a robust taste and are popular in Mexican cuisine. Like all dried beans, black beans contain protein, iron, calcium and phosphorus; they are especially high in fibre.

beans, broad: A type of shell bean also known as fava beans, they are only in season in spring. The beans contain folate, vitamin B$_1$, zinc and protein. They are also a source of L-dopa, known to fight Parkinson's disease.

beans, white: Rather than being a specific bean, this is a group of beans that includes Great Northern, navy, and cannellini. High in fibre and protein, they also contain folic acid, iron and potassium.

beetroot: Red beetroot get their colour from the phytochemical betacyanin, which is believed to reduce tumor growth. They also contain betaine, which helps protect the heart, and salicylic acid, which has anti-inflammatory properties and are specially high in folate. The phytochemicals in golden beetroot help promote eye health and boost immunity.

blackberries: Their dark purple colour, caused by anthocyanins, helps to lower the risk of some cancers and promote urinary tract health. Second only to blueberries in their antioxidant content, they are also high in vitamin C, potassium, folate and fibre.

blueberries: These native American berries are so high in antioxidant and anti-inflammatory compounds that they are considered "brain food": they contain a range of anthocyanins, which are thought to help fight cancer and have antiageing capabilities. They are available fresh, dried and frozen.

blood oranges: See Oranges.

bok choy: Eaten for both its white bulb and its green leaves, bok choy is a type of cabbage and contains the same cancer-fighting compounds as well as a range of vitamins and minerals.

breadcrumbs: Whether ground from stale bread a few days past its peak (fresh) or bread that has dried completely (dried), breadcrumbs add texture and body to many recipes. Seek out unseasoned crumbs which don't contain added salt, dried cheese or other flavourings.

broccoli: Extremely high in vitamin C (60 g/2 oz) provides 68 percent of the daily recommended intake and even higher in vitamin K, broccoli also contains vitamin A and cancer-fighting phytochemicals. Broccoli sprouts also contain high levels of these compounds.

Brussels sprouts: These miniature green cabbages contain the same cancer-fighting compounds as their larger cousins, and are even higher in vitamin C and K than broccoli; just 4 Brussels sprouts contain 243 percent of the daily recommended intake of vitamin K, which promotes proper blood clotting.

cabbage: The patriarch of the cruciferous vegetable family, cabbage can be found red and green and is high in vitamins C and K, but its real value is its concentration of isothio-cyanates, powerful cancer-fighting compounds. Red cabbage, which is actually purple, contains more vitamin C than green cabbage, along with the antioxidant anthocyanin.

capers: A Mediterranean shrub is the source of these small unopened flower buds. The buds are bitter when raw; once they are dried and packed in brine or salt, they are used to add a pleasantly pungent flavour to a variety of dishes. Capers should be rinsed before use to remove excess brine or salt.

carrots: One carrot provides a whopping 330 percent of the daily recommended intake of vitamin A, which is the source of its fame as a protector of eye health. Carrots are also high in fibre and the bioflavonoids and carotenoids that lower the risk of

some cancers, protect the heart and boost immunity. Maroon and purple carrots are colourful alternatives to the common orange carrot, offering different phyto-chemical benefits, and these colours of carrot are becoming more widely available.

cashews: See Nuts.

cauliflower: Another member of the cruciferous family, cauliflower, traditionally, was blanched, or covered during growing, to keep the head white; now it has been bred to be naturally white. Even so, it still contains the cancer-fighting compounds of its cousins, along with phytochemicals that promote hearth health. Purple cauliflower offers a colourful change of pace from the common white cauliflower.

celery: Like other green vegetables, celery helps to fight certain cancers, promotes eye health, strengthens the immune system and helps build strong bones and teeth. It is also high in fibre.

cheese, feta: Young cheese traditionally made from sheep's milk and used in Greek cuisine. It is known for its crumbly texture; some versions are also creamy. Feta's saltiness is heightened by the brine in which the cheese is pickled. Feta is also produced from cow's or goat's milk. Reduced-fat feta is also available.

cherries: Tart red and sweet dark red cherries derive their colour from anthocyanin pigments and other antioxidants, which help protect the heart and brain, lower the risk of some cancers and are powerful anti-inflammatories. Both sweet and tart cherries also contain a terpenoid that appears to prevent the growth of tumours.

chervil: This springtime herb is reminiscent of parsley and anise. It goes particularly well with vegetables, including carrots and asparagus.

chicken stock: Most commercial brands are high in sodium and may contain MSG, sugar and other ingredients. When shopping, look for varieties that are organic or free-range as well as natural, low-sodium and fat free.

chillis: All chillis contain the phytochemical capsaicin, which gives them their hot taste and also acts as a cancer fighter. Although usually eaten only in small amounts, they are nutrient rich, containing vitamins A, C and E, along with folic acid and potassium. Long, brownish red, dried guajillo chillis are widely used in Mexican recipes and have a sharp flavour. Dark burgundy anchos are the dried form of fresh poblano chillis. They have a sweet, chocolatey, fruity flavour.

Chinese broccoli: Called gai lan or Chinese kale, this cruciferous vegetable has slender, crisp stems and dark, blue-green leaves. Sometimes it has small white flowers. It is a good candidate for steaming or blanching and then stir-frying. Look for it at Asian groceries and speciality-food stores.

chives: These slender, bright green stems are used to give an onion-like flavour without the bite. The slender, hollow, grasslike leaves can be snipped with a pair of kitchen scissors to any length and scattered over scrambled eggs, stews, salads, soups, tomatoes or any dish that would benefit from a boost of mild oniony flavor. Chives do not take well to long cooking—they lose flavor and crispness and turn a dull, greyish green.

chocolate: Because chocolate is a plant food, it also contains phytochemicals, in the form of a group of antioxidants called catechins, also found in red wine. Dark chocolate is higher in these flavonoids (and lower in fat and sugar) than milk chocolate.

cinnamon: The dried bark of a tropical tree, the essential oils of this fragrant spice may serve as an anti-inflammatory, prevent the growth of bacteria and help diabetics regulate their blood sugar by boosting their response to insulin. Cinnamon also contains manganese, fibre, iron and calcium.

coconut: The world's largest nut, coconuts contain a fleshy, white, edible interior and sweet, watery liquid that contains fibre, anti-oxidants, vitamins and minerals. Coconut meat is sold flaked and shredded, but often sweetened. Look for unsweetened coconut in speciality-food or health-food stores.

coffee: Like all plant foods, coffee contains beneficial phytochemicals. It is also high in the stimulant caffeine, which some people are sensitive to but which is being studied for its effects countering Parkinson's disease and diabetes.

coriander: This is a distinctly flavoured herb with legions of loyal followers. Used extensively in the cuisines of India, Egypt, Thailand, Vietnam and China, coriander asserts itself with a flavour that can't be missed. Coriander is thought to help rid the body of toxins such as lead and mercury as well as combat anxiety.

corn: Corn is rich in vitamins, minerals, protein and fibre. Yellow corn is given its colour by carotenoids that not only fight heart disease and cancer, but also protect against macular degeneration.

courgettes: Most of the nutrients in courgettes are found in their skin, which contains phytochemicals that strengthen the eyes, bones and teeth; help to boost immunity; and lower the risk of some cancers.

couscous: A pasta made from high-protein durum wheat, couscous is also available in whole-wheat form, which cooks just as quickly and is virtually indistinguishable from regular couscous.

cranberries: High in both fibre and vitamin C, cranberries are excellent for

preventing urinary tract infections due to their polyphenols. The anthocyanins that make cranberries red have antioxidant properties that protect the heart and may guard against cancer. Fresh, frozen and dried cranberries, as well as cranberry juice, are all equally beneficial to your health.

farro: This ancient, unhybridised wheat from Italy is ground and used to make dark, nutty-tasting pasta. The whole grain is also used in soups and salads. You can find it in speciality-food stores and Italian markets.

figs: Whether fresh or dried, figs provide phosphorus, calcium and iron.

flaxseed: An excellent source of omega-3 fatty acids, these mild, small, reddish brown or deep amber seeds have a crunchy outer shell. They not only help prevent heart disease, but also fight breast and colon cancers and contain calcium, iron, niacin, phosphorous and vitamin E. Refrigerate the seeds and oil to keep them from spoiling.

garlic: Unusually rich in antioxidants and anti-inflammatories, garlic forms organosulfur compounds when chopped, crushed or sliced. These substances lower blood pressure, slow clotting and promote heart health.

ginger: Found most often in Chinese cuisine and prized for its culinary and medicinal uses, ginger helps the body with digestion and lowers cholesterol. It contains both antioxidant and antimicrobial compounds.

grapefruit: Half a grapefruit provides 70 per-cent of the Daily Value of vitamin C. Pink or red grapefruits are high in vitamin A as well. Both yellow and pink types contain flavonoids that help guard against cancer, while the latter also has lycopene which boosts that activity.

grapes: The dark purple Concord grape, which is usually made into grape juice,

is extremely high in antioxidants, making grape juice an important heart-healthy food. Red table grapes also promote heart health and immunity, and green grapes can help lower cancer risk and promote eye health.

green beans: Providing both vitamins A and C, green beans also protect eye health because of their lutein content. Long, skinny green beans known as long beans or yard beans are commonly used in Chinese stir-fries. They have a chewier texture and more intense taste than other green beans, which makes them a good match for spicy seasonings.

jicama: Technically a legume, crisp and nutty jicama is eaten both raw and cooked. It provides vitamin C and potassium. It is mainly used in Asian cuisine and may be found in speciality Asian shops.

kasha: The tan-colored, pyramid-shaped roasted seeds of buckwheat, kasha has a pleasantly sour, nutlike taste and robust texture. It is high in protein.

kohlrabi: A member of the turnip family and also known as a cabbage turnip, this crisp, mildly sweet vegetable looks like a regular turnip and tastes like a mildly sweet form of broccoli or cabbage. It is a good source of potassium and vitamin C.

leeks: By virtue of their membership in the onion family, leeks contain organosulfur compounds, which are thought to fight cancer and heart disease. They also help improve the body's good-bad cholesterol ratio.

lemongrass: A long, fibrous, greyish green grass with a paler bulblike base and mild lemon fragrance and citrus flavor, lemon grass is a staple herb of Southeast Asia.

lemons: High in vitamin C, lemons are a flavour enhancer; add lemon juice to raw and cooked fruits and use it to replace salt at the table for vegetables and fish.

lentils: High in protein, like all beans, lentils come in a wide variety of colours. They also provide iron, phosphorus, calcium and vitamins A and B.

lettuces: The many types of lettuce can be divided into four major groups: butterhead, crisphead, leaf, and romaine (cos). Most lettuces are high in vitamins A and C; they also provide calcium and iron. The darker the green of the lettuce, the higher the level of its beneficial phytochemicals, which include the eye-protectant lutein.

limes: High in vitamin C, like all citrus fruits, the juice of the lime also contains lutein, which benefits eye health.

long beans: See Green Beans.

mint: A refreshing herb available in many varieties, with spearmint the most common. Used fresh to flavour a broad range of savoury preparations, including spring lamb, poultry, and vegetables or to decorate desserts.

mushrooms: Not vegetables or fruits but fungi, mushrooms come in a variety of forms and are available both wild and cultivated. They are rich in riboflavin, niacin and pantothenic acid, all B-complex vitamins, and also contain the valuable minerals copper and selenium.

nectarines: Not a hybrid but a relative of the peach, the nectarine has an edible skin that contains many of its phytochemicals. Yellow nectarines contain beta-carotene, while the pink-skinned, white-fleshed variety has its own group of beneficial compounds.

nuts: High in fibre, nuts also contain folate, riboflavin and magnesium. They are high in beneficial omega-3 fatty acids and vitamin E, an antioxidant that protects

brain cells, promotes heart health and lowers LDL (bad) cholesterol. Each specific variety has other benefits as well. Almonds are a good sources of potassium and their skins contain important antioxidants. Walnuts contain ellagic acid, an important disease and cancer fighter, as well as melatonin, an antioxidant that helps you sleep. Cashews also contain copper, to help your body utilise iron and zinc, which helps regulate your metabolism.

okra: A slender, greyish green, ridged pod that contains numerous small, edible seeds, okra has a mild flavour similar to green beans. When cooked, it has a viscous quality that helps thicken soups such as gumbo. It is high in fibre and a good source of vitamin C, folate and magnesium.

olives: One of the world's oldest growing crops, olives have helped sustain people in the Mediterranean for thousands of years. Too bitter to eat when fresh, olives are either pressed to make oil, which is prized for its high levels of vitamin E and heart-healthy monounsaturated fats, or cured.

onions: All onions contain organosulfur compounds that are thought to fight cancer and to promote heart health. Onions also contain quercetin, which boosts these actions, while red onions have the added benefit of the antioxidant anthocyanin.

oranges: Famed for their high vitamin C content, oranges are also high in folate and potassium. They also provide limonoids and flavonoids, two disease-fighting antioxidants. Blood oranges have dramatic red flesh and juice, as well as a flavour reminiscent of berries.

papayas: With flesh ranging from yellow to orange to red, depending on their type, papayas are high in antioxidant carotenoids, which guard against certain cancers.

parsley: With its refreshing, faintly pepper flavour, this bright herb adds vibrant colour and pleasing flavour to almost any savoury dish. Flat-leaf parsley is preferred for cooking for its superior flavour.

passion fruit: Named by a missionary for the Passion of Christ rather than for any earthly romantic feelings, this aromatic fruit has a tart, tropical flavour. Passion fruits are ripe when their inedible skins are wrinkled. Choose one that feels heavy for its size. The pulp and seeds are the parts you eat.

peaches: While its fuzzy skin is usually not eaten, the yellow or white flesh of the peach contains the vitamins A and C. Peaches are available fresh, dried and tinned.

peanuts: Although they are not truly nuts, but legumes, peanuts are high in fat. They are a good source of protein, but they should be eaten in small amounts. Like most nuts, the fat they contain is largely monounsaturated.

pears: The beneficial pigments of pears are concentrated in their skin; as the skin is quite thin (except in the tan-skinned varieties), they can be eaten unpeeled, whether raw or cooked. The flesh contains vitamin A, as well as some phosphorus.

peas: Sometimes called green, or garden, peas, they are best just after picking; they are also available frozen and provide niacin and iron, along with vitamins A and C.

pea shoots: Fresh pea shoots are the young greens and tendrils from the tips of edible pea plant branches. They may be found at farmers' markets in the spring and carry the same nutritional value as regular peas.

peppers: All peppers are high in cancer-fighting phytochemicals; the various compounds that give them their different colours also promote eye health (green, yellow, orange, and red); the anti-oxidants in purple peppers aid memory function and promote healthy ageing. Red peppers are high in vitamin C.

persimmons: Both the small, squat variety, which is eaten when hard and crisp, and the larger, slightly pointed type eaten when fully ripe, are rich in beta-carotenes and vitamin C.

pineapples: The pineapple's sweet, juicy flesh provides manganese, vitamins A and C, and bromelain, an anti-inflammatory enzyme that is also a digestive aid. The tough waxy rind may be dark green, orange-yellow or reddish when the pineapple is ripe.

plantains: A plantain tastes like a less sweet, blander version of its close relative the banana. Its high starch content allows it to be cooked in many ways, and often neutral flavour allows it to pair well with a wide variety of ingredients.

plums: The edible skin of the plum, which comes in a variety of colours, contains most of its phytochemicals, although the yellow, purple or red flesh also contains beneficial compounds. A good source of vitamin C, plums are one of the most healthy fruits. When they are not in season, enjoy them as prunes, their dried form.

pomegranates: The fleshy seeds of this fruit are high in vitamin C, potassium and heart-healthy anthocyanins. The fruit is in season during the autumn months, while pomegranate juice is available year-round in natural foods stores and some other markets.

potatoes: The deeper the color of its pigment, the more healthful phytochemicals a potato possesses, but all potatoes are extremely rich in vitamins and minerals if eaten with the skin; they are also high in fibre. Be sure to buy organic potatoes; commercially grown potatoes may contain high levels of pesticides.

prunes: These dried prune plums, now also called dried plums, are rich in vitamin A, potassium and fibre. They are higher in anti-oxidants than any other fruit or vegetable, making them a top antiageing food.

quinoa: An ancient Incan grain, quinoa is higher in protein than all other grains, and its protein is complete. It is also rich in nutrients and unsaturated fat.

radicchio: A red-leafed member of the chicory family, radicchio has an assertive, bitter flavour and provides beneficial antioxidants such as anthocyanins and lycopene. Radicchio may be eaten raw, grilled, baked or sautéed.

raisins: Antioxidant rich, raisins are also high in vitamins, minerals, and fibre. Both dark raisins and sultanas start as green grapes, but sultanas are treated to prevent oxidation.

raspberries: Red raspberries have more fibre than most other fruits; they are also high in vitamin C and folate and extremely high in cancer-fighting antioxidants. Golden raspberries are much less common, but they contain heart- and eye-healthy bioflavonoids. Although fresh raspberries can be a bit fragile, frozen unsweetened raspberries retain their flavour and are available year-round.

rhubarb: These tart red stalks are one of the first signs of spring in the market. High in vitamin A and beneficial phytochemicals, rhubarb helps protect the heart, boost the immunity and lower the risk of some cancers.

rice, brown: This whole grain retains its bran covering, making it high in fibre. Brown rice is available in long-, medium-, and short-grain varieties. Like other whole grains, it is high in fibre and selenium; because the bran can become rancid at room temperature, brown rice should be kept refrigerated.

rocket: A peppery green, rocket is eaten both cooked and raw. It is a good source of iron and vitamins A and C and contains lutein, which protects eye health.

rosemary: Used fresh or dried, this Mediterranean herb has a strong, fragrant flavour well suited to meats, poultry, seafood and vegetables. It is a particularly good complement to roasted chicken and lamb.

savoiardi buscuits: An Italian biscuit similar to ladyfingers, these oblong biscuits are similar to light, sweet sponge cakes, although their texture is not as moist.

sesame seeds: Flat and minute, sesame seeds come in several colours, but are most commonly light ivory. They are rich in manganese, copper and calcium, and also contain cholesterol-lowering lignans. Because they have a high oil content, they should be kept refrigerated. Toasting them briefly in a dry frying pan brings out their flavour.

shallots: Another onion family member, the shallot contains the same heart-healthy organosulfides as its relatives. It is milder in taste and more convenient to use in small amounts than the onion.

spinach: High in a multitude of nutrients, from vitamins A, C, and K to folate and potassium, spinach is also one of the best sources of lutein, the carotenoid that prevents macular degeneration.

squash, summer: Most of a summer squash's nutrients are contained in its bright, edible yellow skin. It is a good source of manganese, as well as the carotenoids that give it its color.

squash, winter: The dense, meaty flesh of winter squashes is rich with vitamins A and C, folate, manganese and potassium, as well as heart-protective and cancer-fighting carotenoids.

strawberries: Rich in antioxidant content, partly due to their anthocyanin pigments, strawberries are also extremely high in vitamin C. Because of these compounds, as well as their phenolic acids, these berries are thought to be important cancer-fighters.

sunflower seeds: These mild, nutty tasting seeds are high in polyunsaturated fats and vitamin E. They also contain magnesium, which is essential for healthy bones and providing energy, and selenium, an important cancer-fighting mineral.

swedes: This coarse-skinned root vegetable has a mild-tasting orange flesh. It contains vitamins A and C, as well as fibre and potassium.

sweet potatoes: The most commonly available of these root vegetables are a pale yellow variety and a dark orange one often erroneously referred to as a yam. Both are high in fibre, vitamins A and C, and a host of other vitamins and minerals, as well as more beta-carotene than any other vegetable.

Swiss chard: Another member of the far-flung cruciferous vegetable family, chard has dark green leaves and either white, yellow or red stalks and ribs. Along with cancer-fighting phytochemicals, it contains iron and vitamins A and C.

tomatillos: Sometimes called Mexican green tomatoes, tomatillos are firmer and less juicy than tomatoes and grow inside a pale-green papery sheath. Used both raw and cooked, they are an essential ingredient in many Mexican green sauces. Look for tinned tomatillos in speaclist groceries.

tomatoes: Not only are tomatoes high in vitamin C, they are also high in fibre and have good amounts of other vitamins and minerals. Tomatoes also contain lycopene, which lowers cancer risk. The body absorbs this antioxidant better when tomatoes are cooked, making tomato sauce and tomato paste especially healthful.

turnips: With crisp white flesh and a purple cap, this root vegetable has a mild, sweet flavour when young and is woodier with age.

vinegar: Many types are available, made from a variety of red or white wines or, like cider vinegar and rice vinegar, from fruits and grains. Vinegars are further seasoned by infusing them with fresh herbs, fruit, garlic or other flavourful ingredients. All offer a healthy, and low-fat way to season and flavour a wide range of foods.

walnuts: See Nuts.

water chestnuts: Water chestnuts are walnut-sized, dark brown tubers grown in ponds, streams and rivers. The white flesh inside this vegetable is sweet and slightly starchy with a crunchy texture. Tinned water chestnuts should be rinsed before using.

wheat germ: The germ is the embryo contained within every whole grain, or the part that would grow if it were planted and watered. Oil-rich wheat germ is rich in nutrients and often found in all whole-wheat products.

wine: The colours of red and rosé wines are due to the skins of the purple grapes used to make the wines; red wine has more beneficial flavonoids than grape juice. These phytochemicals have been shown to help increase "good" HDL cholesterol.

yoghurt: The bacterial cultures in yoghurt are prized as an aid in digestion. Like the milk it is made from, yoghurt can be full fat, low fat, or fat-free.

Index

A

Almonds, 137
Amaranth, 134
  Popped Amaranth, 118
Antioxidants, 12
Apples, 134
  Pork Chops Smothered in Onions
    & Apples, 63
Apricots, 134
  Apricot-Stuffed Chicken Breasts, 78
Artichokes, 134
  Fettuccine with Broad Beans, Artichokes
    & Asparagus, 48
Asparagus, 134
  Fettuccine with Broad Beans, Artichokes
    & Asparagus, 48
  Purple Asparagus with Orange
    Vinaigrette, 23
  White Asparagus Mimosa with
    Browned Butter, 59
Aubergines, 136
  Aubergine Caponata, 28
  Sichuan Beef with Aubergine, 30

B

Bananas, 134
  Bananas with Cinnamon-Chocolate
    Drizzle, 70
Basil, 134
Beans, 134, 136
  Black Bean & White Corn Salad, 123
  Dry-Fried Long Beans, 41
  Fettuccine with Broad Beans, Artichokes
    & Asparagus, 48
  White Beans with Tomato & Bacon, 118
Beef
  Rib Steak with Red Wine Pan Sauce
    & Bronze Onions, 102
  Sichuan Beef with Aubergine, 30
Beetroot, 134
  Swede & Golden Beetroot
    with Pomegranate Seeds, 84

Blackberries, 134
  Blackberry Crêpes, 34
  Duck with Purple Cabbage, Blackberries
    & Port, 27
  Savoury & Spicy Blackberry Sauce, 28
Blueberries, 134
  Blueberries with Lemon, 29
  Salmon with Wild Blueberry & Rhubarb
    Sauce, 24
Blue recipes. See Purple & blue recipes
Bok choy, 134
  Hot & Sour Bok Choy, 65
Bread
  crumbs, 134–35
  Warm Tomato & Olive Bruschetta, 95
Breakfast Topping, Crunchy, 119
Broccoli, 135
  Red Wine Spaghetti with Red Pepper
    & Onion, 95
  Stir-Fried Chicken with Broccoli
    & Mushrooms, 41
Brown recipes, 13, 110, 133
  Black Bean & White Corn Salad, 123
  Cashew Chicken Stir-Fry, 117
  Crunchy Breakfast Topping, 119
  Ginger Couscous with Dried Fruit, 113
  Kasha with Walnuts & Pasta, 120
  Lentils with Shallots & Serrano Ham, 123
  Mango Chicken with Toasted Quinoa, 120
  Maple Panna Cotta with Candied
    Walnuts, 124
  Peanut Sambal, 119
  Popped Amaranth, 118
  Tamarind Prawns with Peanuts, 113
  Turkey with Red Mole, 114
  White Beans with Tomato & Bacon, 118
Bruschetta, Warm Tomato & Olive, 95
Brussels sprouts, 135
  Brussels Sprouts with Caper & Lemon, 47
Butter, clarified, 96

C

Cabbage, 135

Duck with Purple Cabbage, Blackberries
  & Port, 27
Purple Cabbage with Raisins, 29
Cake, Toasted Madeira, with Cherries, 106
Capers, 135
Caponata, Aubergine, 28
Carbohydrates, 10, 13, 126
Carrots, 135
  Purple Carrots Glazed with Red Wine, 23
Cashews, 137
Cauliflower, 135
  Sicilian Prawns with Cauliflower
    & Almonds, 60
Cheese
  Chicken Breasts Stuffed with Goat's Cheese
    & Rocket, 42
  feta, 135
  Stuffed Squash Blossoms, 81
Cherries, 135
  Pork Tenderloin with Sour Cherry Sauce, 105
  Toasted Madeira Cake with Cherries, 106
Chervil, 135
Chicken
  Apricot-Stuffed Chicken Breasts, 78
  broth, 135
  Cashew Chicken Stir-Fry, 117
  Chicken Breasts Stuffed with Goat's Cheese
    & Rocket, 42
  Chicken Breasts with Tomatillo Sauce, 45
  Chicken with Caramelised Shallots & Wine, 69
  Chicken with Yellow Peppers
    & Passion Fruit, 81
  Mango Chicken with Toasted Quinoa, 120
  Stir-Fried Chicken with Broccoli
    & Mushrooms, 41
Chillis, 135
Chilli sauce or paste, Asian, 134
Chinese broccoli, 135
  Chinese Broccoli with
    Oyster Sauce, 46
Chives, 135
Chocolate, 135
  Bananas with Cinnamon-Chocolate

Drizzle, 70

Chorizo, Potatoes with Parsley &, 60

Cinnamon, 135

Coconut, 136

Coffee, 136

Coriander, 135

Corn, 136

    Black Bean & White Corn Salad, 123

    Sautéed Summer Squash with Corn, 83

Couscous, 136

    Ginger Couscous with Dried Fruit, 113

Cranberries, 136

    Turkey Tenderloin with Cranberry

        Compote, 99

Crêpes, Blackberry, 34

D

Duck, 137

    Duck with Blood Orange Sauce, 99

    Duck with Purple Cabbage,

        Blackberries & Port, 27

E

Eggs

    Spanish Tortilla with Golden Potatoes, 77

F

Farro, 136

Fats, 10, 17, 127

Figs, 136

    Green Figs with Almond Custard, 52

    Pomegranate-Glazed Figs, 34

Fish

    Lemon Sole with Peas, 48

    Potato Galettes with Smoked Salmon, 59

    Salmon with Wild Blueberry

        & Rhubarb Sauce, 24

    Sautéed Trout with Red Grape Sauce, 96

Flaxseed, 136

French Peas & Lettuce, 46

Fresh Ideas

    Aubergine Caponata, 28

    Blueberries with Lemon, 29

    Brussels Sprouts with Caper & Lemon, 47

    Chinese Broccoli with Oyster Sauce, 46

    Crunchy Breakfast Topping, 119

French Peas & Lettuce, 46

Garlic Chips, 64

Garlic Spinach, 47

Herbed Cherry Tomatoes, 101

Hot & Sour Bok Choy, 65

Hungarian Red Peppers, 101

Pan-Seared Mushrooms, 64

Peanut Sambal, 119

Peppered Yellow Pears with Honey, 82

Pineapple with Preserved Ginger, 82

Plantain with Jalapeño, 65

Popped Amaranth, 118

Prosciutto Grapes, 100

Purple Cabbage with Raisins, 29

Sautéed Summer Squash with Corn, 83

Savoury & Spicy Blackberry Sauce, 28

Savoury Sautéed Persimmons, 83

Warm Ruby Grapefruit Salad, 100

White Beans with Tomato & Bacon, 118

Fruits, 8–9, 11, 12, 16. *See also individual fruits*

G

Galettes, Potato, with Smoked Salmon, 59

Garlic, 136

    Garlic Chips, 64

Ghee, 84

Ginger, 136

Grains, 9, 11, 13. *See also individual grains*

Grapefruit, 136

    Warm Ruby Grapefruit Salad, 100

Grapes, 136

    Prosciutto Grapes, 100

    Sautéed Trout with Red Grape Sauce, 96

Green recipes, 38, 131

    Brussels Sprouts with Caper & Lemon, 47

    Chicken Breasts Stuffed with Goat's Cheese

        & Rocket, 42

    Chicken Breasts with Tomatillo Sauce, 45

    Chinese Broccoli with Oyster Sauce, 46

    Dry-Fried Long Beans, 41

    Fettuccine with Broad Beans, Artichokes

        & Asparagus, 48

    French Peas & Lettuce, 46

    Garlic Spinach, 47

    Green Figs with Almond Custard, 52

    Lemon Sole with Peas, 48

Okra with Yellow Plum Tomatoes, 51

Stir-Fried Calamari & Pea Shoots, 45

Stir-Fried Chicken with Broccoli

    & Mushrooms, 41

Swiss Chard with Lemon & Anchovy, 51

H

Ham

    Ham & Sweet Potato Hash, 87

    Lentils with Shallots & Serrano Ham, 123

    Prosciutto Grapes, 100

Hash, Ham & Sweet Potato, 87

Hash Browns, Red-Hot, 105

Herbs, 17. *See also individual herbs*

Hungarian Red Peppers, 101

J

Jicama, 136

K

Kasha, 136

    Kasha with Walnuts & Pasta, 120

Kohlrabi, 136

    Turkey Fricassee with Kohlrabi, Pears

        & Mushrooms, 63

L

Leeks, 136

Legumes, 9, 11, 13. *See also individual legumes*

Lemongrass, 136

Lemons, 136

Lentils, 136

    Lentils with Shallots & Serrano Ham, 123

Lettuce, 136

Limes, 137

M

Mango Chicken with Toasted Quinoa, 120

Meal planning, 16–17

Meat, 16–17. *See also individual meats*

Minerals, 10–11, 129

Mint, 137

Mushrooms, 137

    Pan-Seared Mushrooms, 64

    Stir-Fried Chicken with Broccoli

        & Mushrooms, 41

    Turkey Fricassee with Kohlrabi, Pears

& Mushrooms, 63

Turnips with Peas & Mushrooms, 69

N

Nectarines, 137

White Nectarines with Tawny Port, 70

Nutrition, 8–13, 126–33

Nuts, 9, 13, 137. *See also individual nuts*

O

Oils, 15, 17

Okra, 137

Okra with Yellow Plum Tomatoes, 51

Olives, 137

Onions, 137

Orange recipes. *See* Yellow & orange recipes

Oranges, 137

Duck with Blood Orange Sauce, 99

Prawns with Papaya & Coconut, 78

Purple Asparagus with Orange Vinaigrette, 23

P

Panna Cotta, Maple, with Candied
Walnuts, 124

Pans, 14–15

Papayas, 137

Prawns with Papaya & Coconut, 78

Parsley, 137

Passion fruit, 137

Chicken with Yellow Peppers
& Passion Fruit, 81

Pasta

Fettuccine with Broad Beans, Artichokes
& Asparagus, 48

Kasha with Walnuts & Pasta, 120

Red Wine Spaghetti with Red Pepper
& Onion, 95

Peaches, 137

Peach Shortcake, 88

Peanuts, 137

Peanut Sambal, 119

Tamarind Prawns with Peanuts, 113

Pears, 137

Butternut Squash & Pears with Rosemary,
87

Peppered Yellow Pears with Honey, 82

Turkey Fricassee with Kohlrabi, Pears
& Mushrooms, 63

Peas, 137

French Peas & Lettuce, 47

Lemon Sole with Peas, 48

Turnips with Peas & Mushrooms, 69

Pea shoots, 137

Stir-Fried Calamari & Pea Shoots, 45

Peppers, 134

Chicken with Yellow Peppers
& Passion Fruit, 81

Hungarian Red Peppers, 101

Red Wine Spaghetti with Red Pepper
& Onion, 95

Wild Rice with Purple Pepper
& Pecans, 33

Persimmons, 137

Savoury Sautéed Persimmons, 83

Phytochemicals, 11, 12, 13

Pineapple, 137

Pineapple with Preserved Ginger, 82

Tamarind Prawns with Peanuts, 113

Plantains, 138

Plantain with Jalapeño, 65

Plums, 138

Stir-Fried Pork with Black Plums, 27

Pomegranates, 138

Pomegranate-Glazed Figs, 34

Swede & Golden Beetroots
with Pomegranate Seeds, 84

Pork

Mu Shu Pork, 66

Pork Chops Smothered in Onions
& Apples, 63

Pork Tenderloin with Sour Cherry Sauce,
105

Stir-Fried Pork with Black Plums, 27

Potatoes, 138

Pan-fried Blue Potatoes with Sage, 33

Potatoes with Chorizo & Parsley, 60

Potato Galettes with Smoked Salmon, 59

Red-Hot Hash Browns, 105

Spanish Tortilla with Golden Potatoes, 77

Prawns

Prawns with Papaya & Coconut, 78

Sicilian Prawns with Cauliflower
& Almonds, 60

Tamarind Prawns with Peanuts, 113

Prosciutto Grapes, 100

Protein, 13, 127

Prunes, 138

Purple & blue recipes, 20, 131

Aubergine Caponata, 28

Blackberry Crepes, 34

Blueberries with Lemon, 29

Duck with Purple Cabbage, Blackberries
& Port, 27

Panfried Blue Potatoes with Sage, 33

Pomegranate-Glazed Figs, 34

Purple Asparagus with Orange Vinaigrette,
23

Purple Cabbage with Raisins, 29

Purple Carrots Glazed with Red Wine, 23

Salmon with Wild Blueberry & Rhubarb
Sauce, 24

Savoury & Spicy Blackberry Sauce, 28

Sichuan Beef with Aubergine, 30

Stir-Fried Pork with Black Plums, 27

Wild Rice with Purple Pepper
& Pecans, 33

Q

Quinoa, 138

Mango Chicken with Toasted Quinoa, 120

R

Radicchio, 138

Sautéed Radicchio with Pancetta, 102

Raisins, 138

Raspberries, 138

Red recipes, 92, 133

Duck with Blood Orange Sauce, 99

Herbed Cherry Tomatoes, 101

Hungarian Red Peppers, 101

Pork Tenderloin with Sour Cherry Sauce, 105

Prosciutto Grapes, 100

Red-Hot Hash Browns, 105

Red Wine Spaghetti with Red Pepper
& Onion, 95

Rib Steak with Red Wine Pan Sauce
& Bronze Onions, 102

Sautéed Radicchio with Pancetta, 102

Sautéed Trout with Red Grape Sauce, 96

Strawberries in Red Wine, 106

Toasted Madeira Cake with Cherries, 106

Turkey Tenderloin with Cranberry
Compote, 99

Warm Ruby Grapefruit Salad, 100

Warm Tomato & Olive Bruschetta, 95

Rhubarb, 138

Salmon with Wild Blueberry
& Rhubarb Sauce, 24

Rice, 138
Rocket, 134
    Chicken Breasts Stuffed with Goat's Cheese
        & Rocket, 42
Rosemary, 138

S
Salads
    Black Bean & White Corn Salad, 123
    Warm Ruby Grapefruit Salad, 100
Sambal, Peanut, 119
Sautéing tips, 14–15
Savoiardi cookies, 138
Seeds, 9, 13
Serving size, 130
Sesame oil, 134
Sesame seeds, 138
Shallots, 138
Shortcake, Peach, 88
Sichuan Beef with Aubergine, 30
Sicilian Prawns with Cauliflower &
    Almonds, 60
Spanish Tortilla with Golden Potatoes, 77
Spices, 17
Spinach, 138
    Garlic Spinach, 47
Squash, 138. *See also* Courgette
    Butternut Squash & Pears with
        Rosemary, 87
    Indian-Spiced Squash with Cashews, 84
    Sautéed Summer Squash with Corn, 83
    Stuffed Squash Blossoms, 81
Squid
    Stir-Fried Calamari & Pea Shoots, 45
Stir-frying, 15
Strawberries, 138
    Strawberries in Red Wine, 106
Sunflower seeds, 138
Swedes, 138
    Swede & Golden Beetroot
        with Pomegranate Seeds, 84
Sweet potatoes, 139
    Ham & Sweet Potato Hash, 87
Swiss chard, 139
    Swiss Chard with Lemon & Anchovy, 51

T
Tamarind, 139
    Tamarind Prawns with Peanuts, 113

Tan recipes. *See* White & tan recipes
Tomatillos, 139
    Chicken Breasts with Tomatillo Sauce, 45
    Turkey with Red Mole, 114
Tomatoes, 139
    Chicken Breasts Stuffed with Goat's Cheese
        & Rocket, 42
    Herbed Cherry Tomatoes, 101
    Okra with Yellow Plum Tomatoes, 51
    Warm Tomato & Olive Bruschetta, 95
    White Beans with Tomato & Bacon, 118
Tortilla, Spanish, with Golden Potatoes, 77
Turkey
    Turkey Fricassee with Kohlrabi, Pears
        & Mushrooms, 63
    Turkey Tenderloin with Cranberry
        Compote, 99
    Turkey with Red Mole, 114
Turnips, 139
    Turnips with Peas & Mushrooms, 69

V
Vegetables, 8–9, 11, 12, 16. *See also individual*
    vegetables
Vinegar, 139
Vitamins, 10–11, 128

W
Walnuts, 137
Water chestnuts, 139
Wheat germ, 139
White & tan recipes, 56, 132
    Bananas with Cinnamon-Chocolate
        Drizzle, 70
    Chicken with Caramelised Shallots
        & Wine, 69
    Garlic Chips, 64
    Hot & Sour Bok Choy, 65
    Mu Shu Pork, 66
    Pan-Seared Mushrooms, 64
    Plantain with Jalapeño, 65
    Pork Chops Smothered in Onions
        & Apples, 63
    Potatoes with Chorizo & Parsley, 60
    Potato Galettes with Smoked Salmon, 59
    Sicilian Prawns with Cauliflower
        & Almonds, 60
    Turkey Fricassee with Kohlrabi, Pears
        & Mushrooms, 63

    Turnips with Peas & Mushrooms, 69
    White Asparagus Mimosa with Browned
        Butter, 59
    White Nectarines with Tawny Port, 70
Wild Rice with Purple Pepper
    & Pecans, 33
Wine, 139

Y
Yellow & orange recipes, 74, 132
    Apricot-Stuffed Chicken Breasts, 78
    Butternut Squash & Pears with
        Rosemary, 87
    Chicken with Yellow Peppers
        & Passion Fruit, 81
    Ham & Sweet Potato Hash, 87
    Indian-Spiced Squash with Cashews, 84
    Peach Shortcake, 88
    Peppered Yellow Pears with Honey, 82
    Pineapple with Preserved Ginger, 82
    Prawns with Papaya & Coconut, 78
    Sautéed Summer Squash with Corn, 83
    Savoury Sautéed Persimmons, 83
    Spanish Tortilla with Golden Potatoes, 77
    Stuffed Squash Blossoms, 81
    Swede & Golden Beetroot
        with Pomegranate Seeds, 84
Yoghurt, 139

BONNIER BOOKS
Appledram Barns, Birdham Road
Chichester, West Sussex PO20 7EQ

Bonnier Books Website
www.bonnierbooks.co.uk

First published in the UK
by Bonnier Books, 2007

WELDON OWEN INC.

Chief Executive Officer John Owen

President and Chief Operating Officer Terry Newell

Chief Financial Officer Christine E. Munson

Vice President International Sales Stuart Laurence

Vice President and Creative Director Gaye Allen

Vice President and Publisher Hannah Rahill

Associate Publisher Sarah Putman Clegg

Associate Editor Lauren Higgins

Art Director and Designer Marisa Kwek

Production Director Chris Hemesath

Colour Manager Teri Bell

Production Manager Todd Rechner

Conceived and produced by Weldon Owen Inc.
814 Montgomery Street, San Francisco, CA 94133
Telephone: 415 291 0100   Fax: 415 291 8841

In collaboration with Williams-Sonoma, Inc.
3250 Van Ness Avenue, San Francisco, CA 94109

A WELDON OWEN PRODUCTION
Copyright © 2007 by Weldon Owen Inc. and Williams-Sonoma Inc.

Set in Vectora

Colour separations by Mission Productions Limited.
Printed and bound in Hong Kong by Midas Printing.

ISBN 13: 978-1-905825-42-4

ACKNOWLEDGEMENTS

Weldon Owen wishes to thank the following people for their generous support in producing this book:
Copy Editor Sharron Wood; Consulting Editor Sharon Silva; Proofreaders Kate Washington and Lesli Neilson; Indexer Ken DellaPenta;
Heather Belt; Leigh Noe; Jackie Mills; and Ryan Phillips.

Additional photography by Ben Dearnley: page 18 (bottom right)

Photographer Dan Goldberg

Photographer's Assistant Shawn Convey

Food Stylist Jen Straus

Assistant Food Stylist Max La Rivière-Hedrick

A NOTE ON WEIGHTS AND MEASURES

All recipes include metric and imperial measurements. Metric conversions are based on
a standard developed for these books and have been rounded off. Actual weights may vary.